LRL

WRITERS AND THEIR WORK

ISOBEL ARMSTRONG
General Editor

BRYAN LOUGHREY
Advisory Editor

Charlotte Yonge

CHARLOTTE YONGE
from a photograph of Charlotte Yonge taken at age 35 years

Charlotte Yonge

Alethea Hayter

Northcote House

in association with
The British Council

First published in 1996 by Northcote House Publishers Ltd, Plymbridge House, Estover Road, Plymouth PL6 7PY, United Kingdom.
Tel: +44 (0) 1752 202368. Fax: +44 (0) 1752 202330.

British Library Cataloguing-in-Publication Data
A catalogue record for this book is available from the British Library

ISBN 0 7463 07810

Typeset by Kestrel Data, Exeter.
Printed and bound in the United Kingdom

Contents

Biographical Outline   vii

Abbreviations and References   ix

1 Steering the Reader: Miss Yonge's Literary Art   1

2 Forming the Reader: Tractarian Role Models   16

3 Icons and Stereotypes   29

4 Historical Imagination   38

5 Social Change: Nostalgia and Acceptance   48

6 The Real Charlotte Yonge?   54

Notes   67

Select Bibliography   70

Index   77

Biographical Outline

1823	Charlotte Mary Yonge born 11 August at Otterbourne, Hampshire, daughter of William Yonge, retired Army officer, and his wife Fanny Bargus.
1827–1836	Educated at home by her parents. Visits to London, Oxford and to her Yonge cousins in Devonshire.
1830	Birth of her brother Julian.
1835	John Keble appointed Rector of Hursley. George Moberly appointed Headmaster of Winchester.
1838	Dedication of new Otterbourne church built by William Yonge. Keble prepares her for Confirmation. Her first book, *Le Château de Melville*, published.
1851	Becomes editor of *The Monthly Packet*.
1853	*The Heir of Redclyffe* published.
1854	Death of William Yonge. *The Little Duke* and *Heartsease* published.
1856	*The Daisy Chain* published.
1857	Visits Ireland. *Dynevor Terrace* published.
1858	Marriage of Julian Yonge.
1860	*Hopes and Fears* published.
1861	*The Young Stepmother* published.
1862	Moves with her mother from Otterbourne House to Elderfield. *Countess Kate* published.
1863	*A History of Christian Names* published.
1864	*The Trial* and *A Book of Golden Deeds* published.
1865	Death of the Kebles. *The Clever Woman of the Family* published.
1866	*The Dove in the Eagle's Nest* published.
1867	*The Chaplet of Pearls* published.

1868	Death of Mrs Yonge.
1969	Visits Normandy and Paris.
1873	*The Pillars of the House* and *The Life of Bishop Patteson* published. Julian Yonge's sister-in-law, the invalid Gertrude Walter, becomes a permanent guest at Elderfield.
1876	*The Three Brides* published.
1879	*Magnum Bonum* published.
1884	Julian Yonge sells Otterbourne House.
1892	Death of Julian Yonge.
1893	Editorship of *The Monthly Packet* terminated.
1897	Death of Gertrude Walter.
1899	Presentation of address at Winchester ceremony for the foundation of the Charlotte Yonge scholarship.
1901	Dies 24 March.

Abbreviations and References

Page references in the text are to the Macmillan editions of Miss Yonge's books listed below (except where otherwise stated) as these are the most easily available today; not to the original editions listed in the Select Bibliography.

Books by Charlotte M. Yonge

BGD	*A Book of Golden Deeds of All Times and All Lands* (1893).
CLLC	'Children's Literature of the Last Century', in *Macmillan's Magazine*, 20 (July–October 1869).
CP	*The Chaplet of Pearls* (1911).
CWF	*The Clever Woman of the Family* (1892).
DC	*The Daisy Chain* (1901).
HCN	*History of Christian Names*, 2 vols (1884).
HF	*Hopes and Fears* (1860).
HR	*The Heir of Redclyffe* (1906).
LBP	*Life of John Coleridge Patteson, Missionary Bishop of the Melanesian Island* (generally known under the shortened title *The Life of Bishop Patteson*), 2 vols (1875).
LL	*Love and Life: An Old Story in Eighteenth Century Costume* (1880).
LV	*The Long Vacation* (1895).
MB	*Magnum Bonum or Mother Carey's Brood* (1899).
MCY	*Musings on 'The Christian Year'* (James Parker, 1871).
MYA	*My Young Alcides* (1876).
PH	*The Pillars of the House, or Under Wode, Under Rode*, 2 vols (1889).
PP	*The Prince and the Page* (1909).

SC	*Scenes and Characters, or Eighteen Months at Beechcroft* (1889).
TB	*The Three Brides* (1904).
TC	*The Carbonels*, National Society's Depository (1896).
TG	*The Two Guardians* (1899).
TSS	*Two Sides of the Shield* (1889).
TT	*The Trial* (1865).
WK	*Womankind* (Mozley & Smith, 1881).

Biographies and Critical Studies

BD	Barbara Dennis, *Charlotte Yonge (1823–1901, Novelist of the Oxford Movement: a Literature of Victorian Culture and Society* (Lampeter: Edwin Mellen Press, 1992).
CC	Christabel Coleridge, *Charlotte Mary Yonge: Her Life and Letters* (Macmillan, 1903).
B and L	Georgina Battiscombe and Marghanita Laski (eds), *A Chaplet for Charlotte Yonge* (Cresset Press, 1965).
ER	Ethel Romanes, *Charlotte Mary Yonge: An Appreciation* (Mowbray, 1908).
GB	Georgina Battiscombe, *Charlotte Mary Yonge: The Story of an Uneventful Life* (Constable, 1943).
KY	Kathleen Tillotson, *Mid-Victorian Studies* (Athlone Press, 1965).
M and P	Margaret Mare and Alicia C. Percival, *Victorian Best-Seller: The World of Charlotte Yonge* (Harrap, 1947).
RC	Raymond Chapman, *Faith and Revolt: Studies in the Literary Influence of the Oxford Movement* (Weidenfeld & Nicolson, 1970).
SD	Catherine Sandbach-Dahlstrom, *Be Good Sweet Maid: Charlotte Yonge's Domestic Fiction: A Study in Dogmatic Purpose and Fictional Form* (Stockholm: Almqvist & Wiksell, 1984).

1

Steering the Reader: Miss Yonge's Literary Art

Anyone asked to guess which recently published novel was the favourite reading of young officers in hospital in 1855 in the Crimean War might opt for *Bleak House*, *The Warden*, *The Newcomes*, *North and South*, *Villette* or *Mr Sponge's Sporting Tour* – a dazzling list to choose from. But all would be wrong; the title that headed the young officers' list was Charlotte Mary Yonge's *The Heir of Redclyffe*.

Miss Yonge (as she has always been called by her readers and critics until recently; to call her 'Charlotte', still less 'Yonge', will always seem ludicrous to anyone habitually reading books by or about her) had from the first the knack of involving her readers' personal sympathies. Even her earliest articles, published in children's or church magazines, produced fan letters from clergymen and academics. With the publication of her seventh novel, *The Heir of Redclyffe*, in 1853, her readership dramatically enlarged, and many eminent writers, statesmen, soldiers, shed tears over it. Gladstone, Guizot, Judge Coleridge, Tennyson, Kingsley, Trollope, Lewis Carroll, Christina Rossetti devoured and praised it and its successors. *Heartsease* was the last book Lord Raglan read before his death in the Crimea. George Eliot read *The Daisy Chain* aloud to G. H. Lewes in Florence. Keble, dying in Torquay after a stroke, could read *A Book of Golden Deeds* when he was too weak to tackle anything else. Bishop Patteson's chaplain, at sea in the Pacific after the bishop's murder, consoled his misery by reading *The Chaplet of Pearls*. A midshipman was able to supply from memory a missing page in his ship's copy of *The Daisy Chain*. An officer in the Guards, asked in a game of 'Confessions' what his prime object in life was, answered that it was to make himself like Guy Morville, hero of *The Heir of Redclyffe*.

This novel proved surprisingly influential in providing a role model. The critic George Saintsbury included Guy Morville in an adolescent list of 'Things and Persons to be Adored', together with Sir Launcelot and King Charles the Martyr. William Morris and Edward Burne-Jones, when undergraduates at Oxford, read the novel aloud to each other, chose Guy as the object of their emulation, and took his medieval tastes and chivalric ideals as presiding elements in the formation of the Pre-Raphaelite Brotherhood.

Astonishing comparisons were made between Miss Yonge and some of the greatest writers. She was repeatedly compared with Jane Austen, with Trollope, with Balzac, even with Zola, while Henry Sidgwick, when a Fellow of Trinity, compared her novel *The Trial* with *Madame Bovary*, to the latter's disadvantage; while Flaubert, he said, described only the 'terrible ennui of mean French domestic life . . . Miss Yonge makes one feel how full of interest the narrowest sphere of life is' (ER 93–4).

Many of her contemporary novelists – Louisa Alcott, Mrs Oliphant, Mrs Henry Wood, Rhoda Broughton, George Lawrence – portrayed characters in their novels reacting to Miss Yonge's books. It could be assumed that readers of their novels would need no explanation of such references; Guy Morville and Miss Yonge's other exemplary characters had become a much-loved feature of the general consciousness of readers.

There was of course some contrary opinion. Wilkie Collins made a violent onslaught on Miss Yonge's Puseyite sentimentality.[1] Fitzjames Stephen, in an article on 'The Relation of Novels to Life', suggested that those readers who wept over *The Heir of Redclyffe* were not enjoying a real experience of life, only an 'embodied day-dream'. Edward Fitzgerald said flatly 'I can't read the Adam Bedes and Daisy Chains etc at all'.[2] The equation with George Eliot in his comment is interesting; even those hostile to Miss Yonge's books placed them on a level of greatness that few critics would now discern. Praised or blamed, she was seen as being in eminent company.

Not every reader of Miss Yonge's books wished to emulate or identify with her characters, but nearly every reader enjoyed their company, wished to meet their equivalents in real life, and wanted to know what happened to them next. They seemed as much a part of readers' lives as real-life friends did. The architect William Butterfield was said to be searching for a wife like Ethel May (he remained a lifelong bachelor). Mrs Wilson, wife to Keble's curate, felt personal bereavement at Guy Morville's death. Lonely young girls like Ethel Romanes, later one of Miss Yonge's biographers, found her first real friends in the characters of *The Daisy Chain*. Miss Yonge's mother described an occasion at the Kebles' parsonage when all those present, including Keble himself, passionately discussed why the characters in *The Heir of Redclyffe* behaved as they did, as though they were real-life personages in history.

The living existence of Miss Yonge's characters in the imagination even of her more sophisticated readers is illustrated by Francis Palgrave's famous anecdote of a walking-tour which he and Tennyson made on Dartmoor. Tennyson had a copy of Miss Yonge's *The Young Stepmother* with him, and could not stop himself from reading it even when they were rambling over the moors. At their Princeton inn, Tennyson threw himself down on a huge fourposter bed, with a candle beside him, and read on and on far into the night. One element in the plot of *The Young Stepmother* is that the heroine's husband, Edmund Kendal, a man in his forties with several children, has never been confirmed. At last Palgrave heard Tennyson cry out with satisfaction 'I see land! Mr Kendal is just going to be confirmed', after which he was able to blow out the candle and go to sleep.[3]

Readers worried about the future destiny of Miss Yonge's characters, as Jane Austen's family did about the later lives of Jane and Elizabeth Bennet. Dr Moberly, Headmaster of Winchester and then Bishop of Salisbury, and father of the 'Daisy Chain' brood, made Miss Yonge promise that she would never in any sequel kill off Dr May. Miss Yonge could not resist the many beseeching young fans who wrote for further information about what happened to their favourites; the later destinies of the Mohuns and Merrifields and Somervilles, the Mays and Underwoods, the de la Poers and Umfravilles of her novels in her peak period from the 1850s to the 1870s – the families first encountered in *Scenes and Characters*, *The Castle Builders*, *Heartsease*, *The Daisy Chain*, *the Stokesley Secret*, *Countess Kate*, *The Trial* and *The Pillars of the House* – were revealed, in a whole series of sequels: *Last Heartsease Leaves*, *A Link between 'The Castle Builders' and 'The Pillars of The House'*,

Two Sides of the Shield, Beechcroft at Rockstone, Come to Her Kingdom, Strolling Players, The Long Vacation, Modern Broods – which seeped out, sometimes at first only in small editions to be sold for some good cause, during the eighties and nineties, right up to the last year of her life. Most of the sequels were less convincing, less carefully constructed, than the original stories, but they were keenly seized on by her fans, eager to know the future marriages, offspring, careers of their favourite characters. The process has continued since Miss Yonge's death; like Jane Austen she has had the dubious honour of a sequel to a novel of hers written by another hand, that of Mrs Hicks Beach in *Amabel and Mary Verena*. The world she created has so much autonomous reality that her devoted readers cannot accept that it has no future history.

It is plain, therefore, that in the art of creating memorable fictional characters, Miss Yonge was triumphantly successful. How was it done? Some critics have suggested that she worked without conscious literary art, simply by intuition and watchful observation, which gave her a psychological penetration beyond her rational reach. 'When her imagination stirs, she knows more than she knows that she knows' as K. M. Briggs put it (B and L 20). She herself did not claim to have complete control of the creative process. 'I have taken a sheet of paper and turned my *dramatis personae* loose upon it to see how they will behave' (CC 175) she told a friend, and she was sometimes surprised at how her characters turned out, and how one of them who was intended to be the central figure in a book she was writing could move back as the focus began to concentrate on another character. She even spoke of having just 'found out' the motivation behind a scene which she had previously described (CC 184).

Nevertheless it cam be shown that her command of her art was the result of fully worked out strategies. Basing herself on her own experience, she adopted a formula on which her imagination had dwelt ever since she was a child, and to which her strong power of observation of external events in her life produced valid evidence: the formula of personality development within the framework of a large family group. This was the structural pattern within which she built all her novels about her own times, the 'family chronicles', best known and best loved of all her books. It was not her exclusive discovery and province; she was often compared with Trollope for using this starting-point, the world of the upper-middle-class families of the squirearchy and the professions, but it was far more central to her art and purpose than to his. The formula had already imposed itself on her imagination when she was 'an almost solitary child, with periodical visits to the Elysium of a large family'. To such a child, as she explained late in her life, 'it was natural to dream of other children and their ways and sports till they became almost realities' (*SC* p. vii). So she made up a family of ten boys and eleven girls living in an arbour of the garden, with whom her mind played on solitary walks and at every leisure moment. These imaginary siblings were given substance by her observation of real-life prototypes, the numerous Yonge cousins in Devonshire to whom she paid her 'Elysian' annual visits, and later on by another huge family, the children of George Moberly, Headmaster of Winchester, dear friends of Miss Yonge who were thought to be so obviously the originals of some of her fictional characters that they became known collectively as 'the daisy chain'. Many suggestions have been made that Miss Yonge modelled Guy Morville on Hurrell Froude, and Ethel May on Elizabeth Wordsworth, first Principal of Lady Margaret Hall, or that she appropriated characters from other people's books – Guy Morville from Malory and de la Motte Fouqué, Elinor and Lilias in *Scenes and Characters* from Elinor and Marianne Dashwood in *Sense and Sensibility*. Probably her most frequent model was herself; there are self-portrait elements in Ethel May, in Countess Kate, in Honora Charlecote in *Hopes and Fears*, even in Bessie Merrifield, the only professional novelist Miss Yonge ever portrayed in a novel.

In fact Miss Yonge, like all experienced novelists, used different facets of her friends and acquaintances as pieces in a mosaic when building up her characters; she did not reproduce whole photographs. Some personality trait, particularly a developing one, encountered in real life or in her reading, would seize on her imagination with what she called an idea's 'tyrannous power of insisting on being worked out' (*MYA* p. v). She might keep it in cold storage, to use years later when she could bring wider reading and more mature thought to its embodiment in fiction. The themes that interested her above all were those of human beings, specially the young, developing as they responded to challenges, pursued quests and achieved reconciliations, scrutinizing their own

5

motives as they did so. In the preface to *The Daisy Chain* she defined in the simplest terms her chosen formula for conveying this theme: 'a Family Chronicle, a domestic record of home events, large and small, during those years of early life when the character is chiefly formed . . . an endeavour to trace the effects of those aspirations which are a part of every youthful nature'.

It was the small events, rather than the large ones, which were her focal points. Lettice Cooper (B and L 34–6) maintained that it is by violent dramatic events 'outside the ordinary run of domestic life' that Miss Yonge's stories grip their readers, and it is true that the novels contain a fair sprinkling of carriage and rail accidents, shipwrecks, epidemics, even one murder. But these are no more than can be paralleled in the diaries and memoirs of her real-life contemporaries: Dickens's rail crash, Mrs Carlyle's carriage accident, the drowning at sea of Mrs Browning's brother, the bereavement of Archbishop Tait who when Dean of Carlisle lost five of his six daughters from scarlet fever within a month. Miss Yonge's build-up of plot and characterization depends less on these sensational events than on the accretion of her characters' reactions to the small rituals and disturbances of life in a large family: on in-jokes, daily routines, observance of mourning, the lack of privacy, competing claims on time and attention, sibling loyalties and rivalries, parental discipline and filial obedience or rebellion. She lays no exclusive emphasis on sensational events as tests of her characters, who are shown as equally challenged by the minor disappointments, misunderstandings and embarrassments within the family group, on which she succeeds in conferring as much excitement for the reader as by a heroic rescue or a cholera outbreak.

The techniques, the narrative arts, by which she aroused and directed this excitement were her uses of imagery, plotting and, above all, dialogue; to a lesser extent, by her style and vocabulary. She was a hard-working professional in her approach to her art. Her enormous output might suggest that she tossed off her books without revision, but this is not so. She believed that re-writing was 'the only way to do more than ephemeral work, for it is nearly impossible to get language, character, and keeping all right at first, and re-writing is the only way to be free of useless words and excrescences'. Her family told her that 'reading aloud a first and second copy of mine is like going over a stony or smooth road . . . I generally go back and do over my yesterday's work, much like the snail of the arithmetical problem, who climbed four feet each day and slipped back three each night, besides sometimes going back to write whole masses over again, and get them into keeping or abridge them, but then I am happier re-writing than blocking out' (GB 113–14).

Her most straightforward method of directing her readers' attention to her underlying theme was by explicit signposting in prefaces to her novels, or by giving them, specially in her early work, subtitles which summarized the theme: 'Self Control and Self Conceit', 'Domineering', 'Aspirations', 'A Chronicle of Mistakes' and so on. But in her best period she used a more subtle allegorical approach, a key image either appearing in the title (*The Daisy Chain, Heartsease, Magnum Bonum, The Pillars of the House, The Chaplet of Pearls*) or recurring in the text so as to focus the reader's attention on her theme. In the very first chapter of *The Heir of Redclyffe* Philip Morville breaks off the camellia bloom from the plant which the heroine is carrying, having insisted on taking the plant away as too heavy for her, just as he is later officiously to break off and destroy her happiness with Guy. The coral cross, once belonging to his dead fiancée, which John Martindale gives to Violet in *Heartsease* is the symbol which sustains her and her son throughout the novel. The game of paper boats with which Geraldine Underwood beguiles her little sister in *The Pillars of the House* foretells the fate in store later in the novel for all the siblings whom the paper boats represent. The vision of the star and the spark in the stubble in *The Dove in the Eagle's Nest* has the same function, and even such mundane details as hooks and fishing in *Hopes and Fears*, or drainage in *The Young Stepmother*, are used as lattices to hold the theme together. 'She was not afraid of symbols' as Raymond Chapman said (RC 74), pointing out that she derived this confidence and freedom in the use of images from her Tractarian training; she passed it on in her influence on the chivalric symbols dear to Morris, Rossetti and Burne-Jones, enshrined in the Pre-Raphaelite movement.

The plots of Miss Yonge's novels have been condemned as clumsy or non-existent by some critics, but also highly praised for their deft intricacy and tension by others. Asked whether novelists did not find plot-making their hardest task, Miss Yonge replied 'All ladies find it so except Miss Austen', and she regarded her inability, compared with Jane Austen or Mrs Gaskell, to arrange her material so as to build up a story as her greatest deficiency (CC 213; SC p. ix). Her advice to an aspiring writer was 'About plots, don't you know how one photographer can so place himself as to make the real objects group themselves into a picture? I think the point is to find the point of view in which events might group themselves' (GB 121). But the choice of angle, of point of view, was a technique which she herself never consistently practised.

She certainly did not yield to the wilder plot improbabilities of some of her female novelist contemporaries which, as will be seen, she enjoyed parodying. On the whole she succeeded in inter-weaving the encounters and destinies of her large casts of characters with a good deal of skill, but her plots do not always cohere or convince; she sometimes sacrifices probability to the moral, or – but more rarely – allows the moral to be endangered by fairness and truth to nature, or has recourse to well-worn plot devices such as killing off parents so that their orphaned children can have more scope to display independent action.

Her most effective technique was her dialogue. She gave herself an extraordinary training for this. She used to keep verbatim records of conversations at which she was present, many of them trivial and uninteresting in themselves, but a useful training of ear and memory, and sometimes an invaluable source for phrases and turns of speech which she could use in her novels. As a result she was able to build up a high proportion of her characterization by dialogue alone. That includes characters not morally approved; her scoffing sons and rebellious daughters are fairly made to sound just as life-like as her dutiful ones. Some critics, while according high praise to her dialogue, think that she included too much; Oliver Elton considered it so good that 'it only needs a little less copiousness, another touch of art, to make it perfect of its sort',[4] while Chapman, with a tinge of male chauvinism, alleges that 'sometimes the dialogue runs on until the reader feels almost physically deafened by such a flow of feminine chatter' (RC 85). Not, it will be noticed, by the masculine chatter which also flows on in the novels; unlike Jane Austen, Miss Yonge did venture to present conversations between men and boys with no women present, and several male critics have conceded that her con-versations accurately record the language of schoolboys better than most male authors could do.

Her style and vocabulary were usually so plain as to escape critical comment. She was particular about punctuation and grammatical correctness, deploring slipshod phrases, repetitions, ambiguities, but she also deplored pompous and inflated prose; she makes good fun in *The Pillars of the House* of the sub-editor who, when Felix Underwood as an apprentice reporter referred to the fire at a local inn, corrected 'the fire' into 'the devouring element'. Her own texts, as she described in *Musings on 'The Christian Year'*, were always vetted by Keble, and there is a detectable note of affectionate irony, beneath the reverence, in her description of how Keble's 'poet-hand' altered her reference to the 'circle' of the sun to the 'orb'. Her preference was for monosyllables and economy of expression, whether she was describing a familiar spectacle like the service for the consecration of Hursley Church:

> There were always more men than women, for Hampshire agriculture and cottage life seems to wear out women much sooner than their husbands, and the white or bald heads always predominated over the black bonnets on the long benches (*MCY* p. xliv).

or whether she was re-creating a distant dramatic event like the murder of Bishop Patteson. She tells how his naked body, with five wounds and a palm leaf on his breast, was pushed out to sea in a canoe by the Melanesian islanders who had killed him. There is only one adjective in the whole passage, the 'placid' smile on the dead man's face. A more propagandist, less truthful, biographer would have talked of 'holy' or 'angelic' smiles; but Miss Yonge faithfully mirrors the eye-witness account of the bishop's chaplain that the dead man's face showed no sign of fear or pain, but looked patient and rather tired as he did when he was asleep. (*LBP* vol 2, pp. 381–2, 384).

When it came to creating, not re-creating, a tragic situation in one of her novels, she could be equally laconic. The scapegrace Edgar Underwood, about to be killed with his little son by Red Indians, says

> Never mind, my brave boy, it can't last long. Shut your eyes and say your prayers (*PH* vol 2, p. 437).

which may be thought more economically moving than half a dozen pious death-beds.

Irony, affectionate or astringent, is a tool of which Miss Yonge made much use. She is often accused of being humourless, and her own dictum – that while an author may make use of 'fun and drollery', it must be with an 'underlying earnestness', and that buffoonery, extravagance and irreverence must be avoided – does suggest a rather limited power of laughter (CLLC 453). Certainly she had no pervading sense of the ridiculous like Jane Austen. She does not often invite her readers to laugh at her characters, though she occasionally calls for a sympathetic smile at favourites like Lady Temple in *The Clever Woman of the Family* who, having at sixteen married a sixty-year-old general and then been widowed, is outraged when a peer, years younger than her late husband, proposes to her: 'At his age, too, one would have thought he might have known better'. More usually Miss Yonge's mockery and dramatic irony are employed to influence her readers' estimate of her characters' actions, to show the futility of unworthy goals and the hollowness of conventional illusions. A particular target for her mockery and parody was the ill-written popular novel, whether romantic, 'silver-fork', or intended to be improving. She had nothing but scorn for the 'commonplace novelists' repertory', the 'pathetic governess style', the ludicrous errors of writers who had not done their homework on period or class, the heavy-handed moralists in whose novels 'it is very dangerous to be too good' because the virtuous children always die; she describes Mrs Sherwood as 'first in the field of pious slaughter' (CLLC 308). Many of the characters in her own novels are shown indulging in these misguided attempts at fiction-writing; Rachel Curtis in *The Clever Woman of the Family* produces *Am I Not A Sister*, a leaden piece of feminist propaganda; Theresa Marstone in *Heartsease* churns out allegories about children's education with titles like *The Folded Lambs* and *Pearls of the Deep*, though she has no practical experience of bringing up children; even Bessie Merrifield, depicted in later novels as a genuinely capable writer, starts her career of authorship with *Clare, or No Home* about a golden-haired but persecuted lost heiress. Miss Yonge believed that such ill-thought-out stories could have a baleful influence on young readers, creating false expectations about real life. This critical point was that of George Eliot's famous 1856 article 'Silly Novels by Lady Novelists'[5] though the two women's general approach could hardly have been more different.

It can be shown with fair certainty that Miss Yonge actually read this article. One of the novels pilloried by George Eliot was *Rank and Beauty, or the Young Baroness*, in which a young girl unexpectedly inherits a peerage in her own right, becoming Lady Umfraville, and dazzles the world by her loveliness and wit. A few years later Miss Yonge published *Countess Kate*, in which a young girl unexpectedly inherits a peerage in her own right – but far from dazzling everybody with her beauty and wit, she is clumsy, obstinate, excitable and inconsiderate, though essentially good-hearted, and she finds her new situation intolerably restrictive. Her surname is Umfraville. In *Countess Kate*, one of the best stories she ever wrote, Miss Yonge combined the parodic purpose of dispelling a harmful illusion with the creation of a vividly real human situation.

Miss Yonge did not confine her mockery to other people's novels. Disconcertingly, she often mocked her own imagery and plots, deliberately sawing off the branch on which she was sitting. Dr May's dream of the daisy chain, key image to the whole novel, could be thought 'silly' if taken too solemnly, pronounces one of the characters in the novel. Geraldine Underwood's paper boats, emblematic of the family destinies, are also mocked by an onlooker as a foolish superstitious omen. Miss Yonge often derides her own plots, and not only those in her earliest work, where she later allowed that it was almost inevitable in a youthful composition that 'there should be a cavalier ancestry, a family much given to dying of consumption, and a young marquess cousin' (*TSS* p. vii). In later novels she allows her characters to say that some just-described scene is 'like a story', or that some dénouement is 'just like a good hero in a book . . . living very happy ever after', or 'like the catastrophe in a religious novel, which the Quarterly Review says always ends by the heroine being rewarded by an evangelical young duke' (B and L 142). To her story of a non-existent daughter of Mary Queen of Scots, she gave the title *Unknown to History*. One critic of Victorian fiction[6] suggests that Miss Yonge was unaware of the irony implicit in her choice of title, but it is seldom safe to assume unconscious irony in her works. She often seems to be reminding herself and her readers not to take her novels, as novels, too seriously, and this raises questions, which need to be examined, about her notions of an author's status and responsibilities.

*   *   *

Apart from what she implied in her novels, she wrote directly about her profession in an 1892 article 'Authorship' (B and L 185–92); in a chapter oddly titled 'Money-Making' in her 1877 manual *Womankind*; and in the cogent series of articles on 'Children's Literature of the Last Century', published in *Macmillan's Magazine* in 1869, in which she examined in detail the author/reader relationship. She analysed carefully the type of reader she was addressing: the middle-class young ladies who were devoted to her 'drawing-room stories', the cottage children with their short attention-span and ignorance of history, the boys who wanted nothing but adventure. But she deprecated over-specialization in catering for particular types of readership, and thought that all young readers should be encouraged to 'stretch up to books above them'. Much of what she had to say about the profession of authorship was practical advice to young writers on how to train themselves for the job and get their works published; there is some mention of the writing methods of established authors like Harriet Martineau, but no reference to her own eccentric method of keeping three books – a novel, a historical study, and a manual on teaching scripture – going simultaneously, and writing a page at a time of each in turn, going on from where she had left off, perhaps in mid-sentence, a remarkable demonstration of her control over her material. She was reticent, too, about her own methods of addressing her readers, perhaps because she had no conscious policy about authorial presence in the novel. There is no discernible system in her variations between omniscient objective narrative, second-hand reporting, interior view and authorial comment, except that interior view is given only into the minds of her major characters. Her use of second-hand reporting of crises in her stories, through dialogue or letters, effortlessly shifts the focus to and from the distance. Her use of authorial comment, particularly in the later novels, was restrained but not apologetic. Authors, she contended, should not be too blatantly intrusive, as in some of the Evangelical books for children, but she reserved the right to drive home a moral when its point might not penetrate by the stroke of more oblique tools.

Was her authorial voice expressing the real meaning and message of what she wrote? A number of attempts have been made to deconstruct Miss Yonge's works, starting perhaps as early as George Eliot's remark that when reading Miss Yonge one 'has a sense . . . of the incomplete narrative which cries out for further exploration'.[7] Miss Yonge herself gave some apparent sanction to such explorations when, commenting on Southey's statement that he did not mean, or even understand, an allegorical interpretation of his *Thalaba*, she said 'I am sure this seems as if poets themselves were not the composers of their works' (CC 177).

In recent years critics, particularly feminist ones, have vigorously studied Miss Yonge's novels on deconstructionist principles. The most thorough survey so far devoted to Miss Yonge as a writer, Catherine Sandbach-Dahlstrom's *Be Good Sweet Maid. Charlotte Yonge's Domestic Fiction: A Study in Dogmatic Purpose and Fictional Form*, makes a detailed exploration of the novels in search of the tension between Miss Yonge's natural creativity and the limitations imposed on it by dogma. This critic sets up an elaborate apparatus of 'mute models', 'compromise models', 'doubles', to demonstrate how Miss Yonge combined the avowed intention and the hidden impulse. The latter is seen as often pushing through to shatter the surface of the former, but Miss Yonge is given credit for at least using various strategies to reconcile her message and her subconscious rebellion against it. Moreover this critic realizes, and warns readers against, the danger of letting twentieth-century ideals of individual emotional development make them doubt the sincerity of Miss Yonge's commitment to Christian duties to society. The supposed dichotomy between Miss Yonge's avowed and subconscious purposes is an opposition in the minds of modern readers, not in Miss Yonge's own mind. In the present secularized culture 'we do not only reject religious assumptions, we no longer understand them', and therefore find them implausible in Victorian novels, but this is a displacement between author and reader, not within the author's own consciousness (SD 21–7, 99–100).

Other feminist critics – more interested in uncovering Miss Yonge's unconscious betrayals than in conceding her possible use of 'compromise models' to reconcile what she thought she meant with what they think she must really have, or ought to have, felt – have suggested that beneath her message of self-devotion to others the reader can detect a secret precaution to preserve the status quo of class and masculine oppression, or an unintentional irony by which self-devotion really meant devotion to herself.[8]

A more thorough exhibition of deconstruction, of the reader ignoring the ostensible meaning and creating a more acceptable one, is Gwen Raverat's robust comment in *Period Piece*: 'I could read *The Daisy Chain* or *The Wide Wide World*, and just take the religion as the queer habits of those sorts of people, exactly as if I were reading a story about Mohammedans or Chinese'. It is a neat piece of irony that Miss Yonge herself knew all about this form of deconstruction, the 'noble art of skip' as she called it, recalling herself as a child reading Evangelical books for children and 'diligently extracting the small sandwiches of story, and carefully avoiding the improving substance' (CLLC 232, 228).

Both Gwen Raverat and Miss Yonge are of course describing how children have always picked out what they need from their reading. The more sophisticated recent attempts by adults to deconstruct Miss Yonge's works in their entirety in search of a more fashionable sub-text which they find acceptable, or think they can discern, beneath the authorial intention, have not seemed very convincing. It is not a case of extracting the pills and then enjoying the jam; the mixture is more like an antibiotic in liquid cordial; the reader cannot swallow one without the other, and may not notice that he is being dosed as well as stimulated. 'She needs to be taken on her own terms if she is to be understood' (RC 83). Her intention is so avowed, so consistently pursued, so congruous with everything that is known about her life and emotions, that the search for hidden agendas is apt to be a fruitless though enjoyable pursuit. Readers today may not share her beliefs, but any attempt to show that she herself did not really hold them simply disintegrates, rather than deconstructs, her work.

Her intention was always firm, but her attitude to the novelist's craft in itself, apart from the message, is less serious and respectful. There is a well-known self-mocking anecdote of her descending to lunch, after a morning spent, as usual, on two books at once, *The Life of Bishop Patteson* and *The Pillars of the House*, and saying 'I have had a dreadful day; I have killed the Bishop and Felix' (M and P 217). Her account of her own evolution as a writer, in *Lifelong Friends*, is curiously tentative, almost apologetic. 'With *The Heir of Redclyffe*, when I was about thirty years old, authorship ceased, in a manner, to be a simple amusement, and became a vocation, though never less of a delight, and I hope I may say, of a conscience'. She never referred to herself as a novelist, or as a writer of fiction. Women in her novels who 'set up for an authoress', rather than simply doing the job for altruistic motives – of getting across a moral message or earning money for their families – are apt to be condemned, and none of her novels has a male novelist as a central figure; she never produced the equivalent of a *David Copperfield* or a *Pendennis*.

In fact, the whole of her craft as a writer – which has been given first place, before any other aspect of her work, in this book because least attention has been paid to it in most studies of her work – would have been given a lower priority by Miss Yonge herself. Her valuation of her own profession of authorship in itself was not supreme in her scale of things; she saw her lifelong pursuit as an almost irresistible temptation, to which it was only justifiable to yield if it served a higher end. That higher end must now be surveyed in the next chapter.

2

Forming the Reader: Tractarian Role Models

Miss Yonge did not write for money or fame. She was sufficiently well off not to need to earn her living, and in fact she gave away most of the royalties from her writing to missionary good causes. Though she enjoyed talking about her books with her friends, she shunned public acclaim; Keble had taught her that fame was a dangerous temptation, so when the undergraduate audience at an Oxford Encaenia greeted her with cheers, she refused to believe that the applause was meant for her, and when a presentation ceremony in her honour was arranged at Winchester, any pleasure she may have felt was concealed by unsmiling embarrassment. She wrote, not for renown or an income, but irresistibly; it was her greatest pleasure in life, but she was fortunate in believing that her highest enjoyment was also her God-given duty, that she was called to testify Pro Ecclesia Dei, which she understood as the Church of England in its Tractarian aspect.

Barbara Dennis, in her thorough and well-researched study, *Charlotte Yonge, Novelist of the Oxford Movement*, has shown how Miss Yonge's forebears and her immediate family belonged to the old High Church Non-Juror tradition, reticently devout; so that Tractarian doctrine, when her parents encountered it, seemed 'nothing new, only the full consequence of what they had always learnt' (MCY p. viii). To their fifteen-year-old daughter, born and educated in this tradition, its 'full consequence' invaded her mind with lifelong ascendancy when John Keble – newly arrived as Rector of Hursley, the neighbouring village to the Yonges' Otterbourne – prepared her for Confirmation. What she learnt from him became the greatest influence of her life, by her own testimony: 'No-one else, save my own father, had so much to do with my whole cast of mind' (*MCY* iii–iv). He imbued her creative imagination with the newly revealed principles of the Oxford Movement, of which he had been one of the founders; he read and corrected the books which she began to write under the stimulus given to her imagination. All her life she was surrounded by a circle of Tractarian friends and acquaintances, chief among them Sir William Heathcote, Bishop Moberly, her close and dominating friend Marianne Dyson, but it was Keble above all who gave muscle to her intellectual grasp of doctrine, and shaped her notions of a Churchwoman's duty. She knew by heart, and uncritically admired as poetry, Keble's *Christian Year* to which after his death she devoted a book of *Musings* – a hard mouthful for even her most devoted admirers and fellow-believers – which contained her frankest and most rigorous statements about her religious doctrines, which in her novels she only allowed to appear by implication, not by direct exposition. Keble had taught her that open preaching of religion, the brandishing of holy names and words, were an irreverence in fiction, and she never directly named Jesus Christ, the Crucifixion, the Eucharist, in her novels.

The Tractarian doctrines imparted to her by Keble, and subsequently underlying her fiction, stressed the efficacy of the Sacraments of Baptism, Confirmation and Communion, the validity of the Apostolic Succession, devotion to the text and rubrics of the Book of Common Prayer, the call to frequent church-going, to church-building, to missionary work, to Sunday school teaching, to the founding of sisterhoods. The extent to which these doctrines and practices permeate the smallest details of her novels can only be appreciated when they are compared with the widespread, though not universal, laxities of the pre-Tractarian Church of England. Fox-hunting parsons; Communion services held only the minimum three times a year, or at best once a month; Matins and Evensong only on Sundays, not daily; a mere 'Service Book' instead of the full Book of Common Prayer; dilapidated churches defaced by coats of arms and stove-pipes – these are the background against which the Tractarian details in Miss Yonge's novels stand out. When a young parson in *Chantry House* gives up field sports 'in deference to higher notions of clerical duty'; when Edward Underwood is attracted by an advertisement for a curate for a parish where there is weekly

Communion; when Mrs Charnock Poynsett in *The Three Brides* is puzzled about Ember Days, which had not been observed in her youth; these passing sentence-long references fill up a whole rich picture of nineteenth-century ecclesiastical change.[1]

The virtues most inculcated by the Tractarians were truthfulness, self-sacrifice, true courage, self-control, filial piety, the humility which scrutinizes and repents the smallest sin. Religious sentiment should be disciplined by will-power, and religious truths should be imparted with reverent reticence, not obtruded. It was this message of the inward life of the mind and soul, the essence of the original Tractarianism, not the ritualistic trappings and practices of its later developments, that influenced Miss Yonge. Under Keble's tuition, she saw a danger that Church ritual, and even doctrine, might be loved merely for their beauty and poetry, an 'aesthetic admiration' which might replace real love and reverence for religious truth. Later in the century she began to feel that the Church had moved into a 'time of decay'. In a curious testament, left unfinished at her death and published posthumously, *Reasons Why I Am A Catholic And Not A Roman Catholic*, she re-stated the true essence of early Tractarianism, which recent converts to Rome had not, in her opinion, really understood (*MCY* pp. v–vi, 253, 313).

This early Tractarianism was the rock-hard foundation which lay below all Miss Yonge's novels, an unseen but essential support. In her earliest novels it was sometimes more visible, in prefaces if not in the main text. Her *Abbeychurch* was designed, she said, to show the need for self-control, *Scenes and Characters* to 'exemplify the effects of being guided by mere feeling, set in contrast with strict adherence to duty', *Henrietta's Wish* to exalt filial submission against wilfulness, *The Castle Builders* to exhibit the dissatisfied life of someone 'not seeking strength and assistance in the appointed means of grace' (*TG* pp. v–vi). The moral framework of *The Heir of Redclyffe* is particularly symptomatic, because it started with an idea supplied by Marianne Dyson which had no inescapable moral implication and could in fact have been observed and used by Henry James. It was to be a contrast between 'the essentially contrite and the self-satisfied', the latter hounding the former to death. When she came to develop this fairly neutral theme, she showed the essentially self-satisfied character, Philip Morville, eventually repenting, thereby adding a message of Christian redemption to the plot. She was always fascinated by the contrast between self-satisfied self-deceivers and the truly humble, and used it again in *The Daisy Chain* with Flora May, in *The Three Brides* and in *New Ground*.

The control of plot by such masterful moral messages, even though implicit rather than avowed in the text, might be thought inevitably to impair the popularity and artistic integrity of Miss Yonge's novels. But such a judgment ignores her technical skill. Where a novelist today might use reactions to such events as redundancy, divorce or drug addiction to illustrate character development, Miss Yonge used loss of faith, conversion to Rome, or worldly cynicism, for the same purpose, and imbued them with quite as much excitement and readability. All the missionary meetings, the retreats, the Church bazaars and fêtes, the Cathedral anthems, the stained-glass windows, in her novels are there for artistic as well as moral purposes – as much as balls or battles are in other writers' fiction – to elicit enthusiasm or boredom, aesthetic rapture or distaste, high resolve or frivolity from her characters.

Moreover she had a unique power to forestall criticism of her novels as mere propaganda. As all commentators on her work have pointed out, she was able to make virtuous characters attractive and interesting too. This is a very rare gift, not granted to novelists of much greater power than Miss Yonge, such as Samuel Richardson and George Eliot. We may admire Sir Charles Grandison and Daniel Deronda, but we scarcely wish to meet them; but it is easy to imagine a really companionable friendship with Guy Morville, Ethel May, Felix Underwood or the Little Duke. Guy, as Professor Tillotson has pointed out, manages to combine unquestionable goodness, even saintliness, with 'a positive Byronic glamour' (KT 53). Even in her own time, when readers were less suspicious of virtuous heroes than they are now, Miss Yonge was apt to be questioned as to whether such saintly characters could be true to life, but she 'never would admit that the heroes of her stories were "too good to be true", but always said she had known as good or better'. They were not ideals, but based on originals she had known in real life, such as Lord Seaton, Warden Barter and of course Keble. The 'religious and conscientious men of the stories had their actual counterparts . . . they were by no means the impossible monsters they are sometimes declared to be', she always insisted (CC 36, 101–2, 303, 337; M and P 235). This conviction of hers enabled her to endow her exemplary characters with a real warmth and sparkle which inclined readers to adopt them as role models. 'Never before did the beauty of holiness appear more beautiful or more winning' said the *Times* reviewer of *The Heir of Redclyffe*, and it was this winning power which was to be Miss Yonge's greatest weapon in her crusade to form the characters of her readers.

What she saw as her mission, being 'a sort of instrument for popularizing Church views' was not, in her novels, carried out by direct preaching but by creating characters whom her readers would like to resemble. It is natural for young readers to want to perform heroic Superman-type feats, and in a whole series – *A Book of Worthies, Biographies of Good Women, A Book of Golden Deeds* and so on – Miss Yonge was to extract from history 'soul-stirring deeds . . . in the trust that example may inspire the spirit of heroism and self-devotion' (BGD pp. v, 9). But in her novels of contemporary life she tackled the far more difficult task of making her readers want to emulate heroism in everyday life, to find glamour in steadfast duty and self-denial. It was perhaps her greatest triumph as a novelist that she was able to make her readers feel that duty was romantically desirable rather than stern.

She was aware, as Carlyle was not, of the dangers of hero-worship, of over-submission to guidance by hero-models, which could turn into idolatry, the setting up of 'Bilds', as she called them. One whole novel of hers, *Hopes and Fears*, was based on the theme that the search for role models may be a detour on the road to holiness. In general, though, she felt confident that she could teach her readers by exhibiting examples who should not be slavishly imitated, but analysed for the motivation which made them so attractively resolute. Her success is witnessed by such testimonies as that of one of her earliest biographers, Ethel Romanes, that Ethel May, heroine of The *Daisy Chain*, 'inspired so many of us to work for the Church' (ER 72), and of Lucy Lyttelton that *The Heir of Redclyffe* and *Heartsease* influenced her girlhood and were permanently enthroned in her memory; they were the first modern novels her parents allowed her to read.[2]

Lucy Lyttelton, daughter of one leading politician and married to another – Lord Frederick Cavendish who was murdered by Irish terrorists – is a prime example of the fairly small but influentially placed group that constituted Miss Yonge's main readership. Chiefly upper-class and upper-middle-class young women, extending from English, German and Italian princesses to curates' daughters, they acquired from Miss Yonge's books an idea of the duty of a Christian woman which issued in philanthropic action, pervading the society of their day, disproportionate to their fairly modest numbers. *The Monthly Packet*, the magazine which Miss Yonge edited single-handedly from 1851 to 1893, and which next to her novels was her main tool in forming the ideals of her readers, never had a circulation much above 1500; it had no staff, no office, no fixed day of publication, no mainstream popularity. Miss Yonge's own family nicknamed it 'The Codger' on the grounds that it was intended to please steady old codgers. Nevertheless it achieved to a considerable extent the aim set out in its opening number: to be a help to those who are forming their characters, 'as a companion in times of recreation, which may help you to perceive how to bring your religious principles to bear upon your daily life, may show you . . . examples both good and evil', may be instrumental in creating 'more steadfast and dutiful daughters of our own beloved Catholic Church of England'. To achieve this aim, each issue of *The Monthly Packet* contained an article on some religious theme, such as Miss Yonge's own *Conversations on the Catechism*, reviews of recommended books, historical sketches, occasional pieces on other subjects such as natural history, onomastics or legendary lore, and a sweetener in the form of a serial story; many of Miss Yonge's novels, including *The Daisy Chain*, *The Trial* and *The Pillars of the House*, appeared first in this form. It does not sound like a formula for promoting mass circulation, nor was it meant to be; it was carefully tailored to fit a special readership, which could then in turn radiate its influence into society in general, in favour of Tractarian aims.

The building and restoration of churches was a Tractarian duty accepted by leading characters in Miss Yonge's novels. She gives a detailed description of St Matthew's Whittingtonia, the church and settlement in London's East End which Robert Fulmort, of *Hopes and Fears*, endowed with the fortune which he had inherited from his gin-distilling father. It was a complex of chapel, school, orphanage and clergy quarters, built of white brick and austerely furnished with wooden benches and matting on the floors. Still more detailed is her description of St Andrew's Cocksmoor, the building of which is one of the central themes of *The Daisy Chain*.

It has a pierced spire with a weathercock, a deep porch, two aisles, a high-pitched roof with exposed oak beams like the ribs of a ship, ancient carved woodwork bought from a chapel in France, and stained-glass windows depicting Saint Andrew, Saint Margaret and the Ship of the Apostles. It was designed by an amateur architect, a local doctor, just as the real Otterbourne Church was designed by an amateur, Miss Yonge's father, but it sounds as though it had been patterned after the work of one of the Tractarian professional architects such as William Butterfield or G. E. Street. Butterfield was an admirer of Miss Yonge's books. She could actually have known Street, who was commissioned in 1865 to restore the Saxon church of St Swithun, Headbourne Worthy, near Winchester, by its rector, my grandfather John Henry Slessor. He was an enthusiast for church restoration, and himself carved much of the woodwork in the restored St Swithun's, including a font-cover with patterns of oak leaves and acorns, ivy, hops, holly, blackberries, grapes, hazel nuts and wild strawberries. His double interest, in church restoration and in botany, and the fact that he had a local reputation as a 'Puseyite priest', seem to make my grandfather into a typical Miss Yonge character, and she could well have known him; Headbourne Worthy, where he was rector from 1861 to 1905, is only a few miles from Otterbourne.

Church restoration is a frequent theme of the family chronicles, from timid attempts in the 1830s by the local squire to pull down choir galleries and reinstate chancels, to the 1890s work of professional decorators frescoing ceilings at the High Church St Kenelm's at a Devonshire seaside resort. Several families in the chronicles inherit country houses which had originally been priories, and which still have their cloisters and vaults and Lady chapels, disfigured and despoiled of their statues and canopies, or reduced to creeper-clad ruins. The restoration of their former Gothic glories is a favourite occupation of the new heirs, and one such owner plans to turn her house back into a combined church and orphanage, though none of them go so far as to restore the buildings to full monastic use.

The monastic life was another Tractarian ideal of which Miss Yonge made use in her novels, as well as supporting it in real life; many of her charitable donations went towards the founding of new sisterhoods, and after her mother's death she contemplated joining the Community of St Mary the Virgin at Wantage, but in the end decided only to become an Exterior Sister, though she often visited Wantage and always found both peace and sparkling eager life there. The mid-nineteenth century saw the foundation of many Anglican sisterhoods such as the Holy Cross order at Park Village in London, the Community of St John the Baptist at Clewer, and the Sisterhood of Mercy at Devonport.[3] It was the practical works of such sisterhoods – teaching, nursing, prison visiting – that impressed her most, perhaps because she herself was more naturally equipped for the contemplative side of convent life; she was bad at nursing, but good at prayer and liturgies. Her fictional convent of St Faith's, Dearport, which reappears in many of her family chronicles, was probably inspired jointly by the Devonport and Wantage communities; it was primarily a nursing order, and its sisters are constantly summoned throughout the novels to help in epidemics and domestic crises.

Miss Yonge gave charitable donations for building church schools and restoring churches, for sisterhoods, for organizations like the Girls Friendly Society, but most of the profits from her books went to support missionary work, which to her was the essence of chivalry and romance. As Barbara Dennis has pointed out, Miss Yonge's novelist contemporaries were apt to portray missionaries as ridiculous, as Dickens did, or as narrow and cold, as Charlotte Brontë did (BD 83–5, 87–100). But Miss Yonge's missionaries are successfully depicted as the height of glamour, and in this she both influenced and represented the ideals of many young men of her age. Mark Girouard has shown in *The Return to Camelot* how the romantic notions of upper- class public schoolboys about medieval chivalry were closely linked with the impulse towards missionary work among the English working class.[4] Edward Burne-Jones's undergraduate project for a religious order to work among the urban poor, which was to have Sir Galahad for its patron, was largely inspired by *The Heir of Redclyffe*. Ruskin's band of road-making Oxford undergraduates, working for the community, and his Guild of St George were bound up with the concept of knighthood aiding the weak. When Miss Yonge wrote, in the preface to *A Book of Golden Deeds*, of young people whose hearts burned within them at hearing of deeds of true glory, and who longed for opportunities to act in the same way, she was both reflecting and appealing to the aspirations of a whole section of her contemporaries, who worked to help the urban poor through Sunday schools, the National Society and its textbooks, temperance movements, gymnasia, cooking classes, orphanages, East End settlements. Miss Yonge's fictional settlement, St Matthew's Whittingtonia, epitomizes all these activities, and Miss Yonge was reluctantly far-sighted enough to trace the evolution from voluntary missions of this kind, under the auspices of the Church, towards the development of the secular professional social worker. Gerald Underwood, son of a sceptical father but brought up by a pious uncle and aunt, appears in one of the late family chronicles as the representative of the 1890s, a Socialist whose chief interest is case-work in the slums and who looks forward to a revolution which would sweep away hereditary estates like his own, and build housing for the poor over its untouched beauty (*LV*, 3, 19, 85, 128).

Deeply interested as Miss Yonge was in missionary work for the urban poor at home, her strongest feelings of romantic excitement were for overseas missions. Hers was the great period of missionary fervour, in which it was a frequent real-life occurrence, not a novelist's dream, that young men should be inspired by a sermon to dedicate their lives to becoming missionaries at the ends of the earth. In her life of Bishop Patteson she related how, with academic success, social popularity, aesthetic tastes, influential family and friends, he would seem to have had everything to tempt him to an easy life in England, but how, ever since he had heard a missionary sermon at Eton, he had longed to dedicate himself to the hard life of a missionary in Melanesia; not merely felt it a duty, but longed for it with yearning enthusiasm (*LBP* vol 1, pp. 90–1). When she made her fictional characters Owen Sandbrook and Norman May give up prosperous positions and promising careers in order to go off as missionaries to Canada and to New Zealand, she was not imagining impossibly noble choices, but was reproducing real-life models. She supported the Society for the Propagation of the Gospel, the Universities Mission to Central Africa, the Melanesian Mission to the Pacific, and other Church Missionary societies, both by her benefactions and by frequent articles in *The Monthly Packet* and two novels, *New Ground* and *The Making of a Missionary* which made mission work their theme. All through her family chronicles, missionary meetings are frequent and highlighted events.

When she exclaims in *The Daisy Chain* 'Who knows not an SPG meeting?', or in *The Long Vacation* tags an address by a New Zealand missionary onto the end of a family wedding, her romantic feelings about overseas missions do rather topple over into absurdity, but on the whole she sustains convincingly the idea that dedication to missionary work was a thrilling role model. Miss Yonge and her friends and mentors occupied an Anglo-Catholic plateau of doctrine and practice, reticent and unostentatious, between the spiky peaks of the Ritualists and the Evangelical lowlands, and in her novels she is equally critical of both extremes of Anglicanism. She mocks the genuflexions and crossings of young women who are 'technically reverent' during actual Church services, but 'gabble up to the very porch'; the over-earnest young parish worker who could talk of nothing but liturgical colours, chants and teetotalism; the women who set up their own religious order of two because they were dissatisfied with the rules of several established sisterhoods they had tried, and go about in habits of their own devising. She also mocks the other extreme, the Evangelical spinsters with their tracts and their objections to the teaching of the Catechism in Sunday schools, their No-Popery terrors and insistence on faith rather than works. The mockery is generally good-humoured, she concedes the good intentions and philanthropy of those whom she mocks. She was at first much less tolerant of actual Dissent, which she regarded with a rather absurd horror; there was no such detailed and affectionately derisive descriptions of whole Dissenting communities in her novels as there are in Mrs Oliphant's, or in George Eliot's *Silas Marner*. Later on she became more tolerant and her few Dissenting characters are credited with genuine piety, though she makes fun of their canting phrases. Conversions to and from various sects and churches are quite frequent among Miss Yonge's characters; several of them go over, or are in danger of going over, to Rome, a Unitarian is converted to Anglicanism, one particularly worldly female eventually joins the Plymouth Brethren, but even she, though not 'embellished' by the dress of the sect, and tending to try and convert all her former associates, however religious they already are, is allowed to be earnest and charitable. Perhaps Miss Yonge's finest display-piece on the subject of conversions is the character of Angela Underwood who, through a succession of the family chronicles, is first a Ritualist, then an Evangelical bordering on Dissent, then a member of a sisterhood, then teetering on the edge of Rome, finally becoming an Anglican missionary in Australia. The novels reveal a whole world of Victorian religious shifts, preoccupations, party attitudes, which hardly appear in most fiction of the period (Mr Arabin's near-conversion to Rome in Trollope's *Barchester Towers* is a notable exception) but which are a necessary background for understanding the spirit of the age.

There is one religious topic which does feature in much fiction of the time, and which Miss Yonge boldly tackles, and that is 'Doubt', the loss of all religious faith. In the age of Darwin, Carlyle, Tennyson, Froude, it was a central preoccupation pervading the press, public opinion, the hopes and fears of the young, much as today's ecological preoccupations with global warming, the destruction of rain forests, and cruelty to animals do. It caused public debates, accusations of heresy or hypocrisy, the abandonment of careers, the break-up of families, the parting of friends. Miss Yonge never devoted a whole novel to it, as James Anthony Froude did in *The Nemesis of Faith* or Mrs Humphry Ward in *Robert Elsmere* (Mrs Humphry Ward was in her girlhood one of the inner circle of *Monthly Packet* readers under Miss Yonge's influence, from which she later moved away). For Miss Yonge so dire a topic as loss of faith would have probably have seemed too dangerous and irreverent for a whole novel, but many of her characters came near to the edge, and some – though none of her female characters – slipped over into the abyss. Clever girls and women like Bertha Fulmort and Rachel Curtis are shown as temporarily bewildered by Doubt, but are soon drawn back into safety by counsellors who can match their intellectual stature. There are others like Barbara Brownlow in *Magnum Bonum* whose dying suitor makes her promise never to read 'those sneering books' which were flippant about religious truths. Tennyson's

> Leave thou thy sister when she prays,
> Her early Heaven, her happy views;
> Nor thou with shadow'd hint confuse
> A life that leads melodious days[5]

would make a suitable chapter-heading for Miss Yonge's passages about women in danger of 'Doubt'.

It was not so simple to give a faithful picture of adult men of intellect losing and regaining their faith. Miss Yonge was honest enough to tackle this difficulty head-on, and to show varying outcomes. In the family chronicles Norman May in *The Daisy Chain* becomes a prey to religious doubt at Oxford, because of the intellectual pride which made him read up both sides of the question in order to defeat an adversary in controversy, but he emerges from the 'bad dream' and becomes a missionary, and eventually a bishop, in New Zealand. Bobus Brownlow, in *Magnum Bonum*, has a long-lasting loss of faith, teaches in a secular Japanese university, publishes atheistic articles in magazines, is made by his brother's mortal illness to feel that 'this universe was one grim, pitiless machine, grinding down humanity by mere law of necessity, or if . . . there was supernatural power, it could only be malevolent' (*MB* 462, 467). His brother's recovery and his fiancée's steadfast faith may reconvert him, but the end of the book leaves this open. Edgar Underwood in *The Pillars of the House* loses his faith less by any intellectual process than by mere flippancy and idle selfishness; he neglects opportunities to be confirmed, and in a wandering life forgets even the words of the prayers and biblical texts that he had once, as a clergyman's son, heard so often. Mortally wounded by Red Indians in the American Far West, he deliriously recalls tags of Scripture but shows no real repentance, and only the brother and sister closest to him, when they finally hear of his death, can believe that he has escaped the damnation which, in Miss Yonge's conviction, must await the unrepentant. She was no Mrs Sherwood, to consign her characters openly to Hell, and the reader is allowed to remain in doubt about the fate of this amusing and attractive character in the life to come.

Miss Yonge's role models for redeemed doubters are perhaps too simplistically hopeful for sophisticated intellectuals struggling with loss of faith. We may doubt whether the real-life Bobus Brownlows of her day would have been brought back into the fold by his fictional example. She had perhaps ventured too far outside her own experience; she may have known in real life men as devout as Guy Morville and Felix Underwood, but her limited circle probably did not include any agnostics.

Miss Yonge's aim of 'popularizing Church views' was blessed with the fulfilment she hoped for. 'She was almost the first story-teller who dared to write of the Religious life as a normal development . . . She had influenced many people who are now themselves old; she has held up to them an ideal of goodness; she has made them know the possibilities within their own Church; she does indeed deserve a place among the leaders of religion in the Church of England . . . No-one who really wishes to know something of the history of that extraordinary revival of life and of devotion in the Anglican Communion ought to ignore Charlotte Mary Yonge' wrote her disciple and early critic Ethel Romanes (ER 3–4). A 1903 obituary of her in the *Guardian* said 'When the history of the great revival of the Church of England is written in completeness, and effects are traced back to causes, and the real actors in that drama emerge, a considerable amount of attention will be given to the work of Miss Yonge. Few women have played a really greater part in a great religious revival' (BD 1). This was a true prophecy, as the aspect of Miss Yonge's work most studied by modern critics has been how Tractarianism pervaded her novels, and how they in turn influenced readers towards Tractarianism.

3

Icons and Stereotypes

Moss Yonge was unlucky in the illustrations to her works. The best of a bad bunch of illustrators was possibly W. J. Hennessy; others were obscure artists such as Herbert Gandy, Adrian Stokes and J. Priestman Atkinson, who contributed some ludicrous images to a 1901 edition of *The Daisy Chain*. But the prize for awfulness must go to Kate Greenaway, whose *Heir of Redclyffe* illustration shows Amy Edmonstone, apparently just about to throw up, and wearing, not the crinoline which would have been appropriate to the 1850s in which the book is set, but the uniquely unbecoming tube dress, with a bow over the crotch, of the early 1900s. Beside her Guy Morville, with a walrus moustache, wears a bowler hat for this love-scene in a rose garden.

It is a pity that some of the better Victorian painters were not enrolled to illustrate Miss Yonge's books; Arthur Hughes, for instance, whose *Long Engagement* with its wistful young lovers in a wood would have made a better accompaniment than Kate Greenaway's monstrosity to the scene of Guy's proposal to Amy. It would indeed be easy and enjoyable to compile a list of familiar Victorian pictures to accompany Miss Yonge's books. One could choose Augustus Egg's *Travelling Companions*, the two sisters in their silvery crinolines facing each other across a railway carriage; Millais's *My First Sermon*, the red-caped child with her muff, alert in a church pew; R. B. Martineau's *The Last Day in the Old Home*; James Collinson's *For Sale*, the woman at a Church bazaar with her ambiguous glance, and so on (though no such notorious icons as Holman Hunt's *The Awakening Conscience* or John Collier's *A Fallen Idol*; Miss Yonge's books contained no fallen woman, no repentant Little Em'ly). These favourite Victorian pictures, endlessly reproduced in prints hung in suburban villas and seaside lodging-houses, stimulated the visual responses of novel-readers of the day. Weeping over the death of Little Nell, they were more likely to visualize her as the girl in James Sant's *The Soul's Awakening*, with her upturned eyes and graceful curls, than as George Cattermole's fat-faced lumpish corpse illustrating the original edition of *The Old Curiosity Shop*. The popular images of the successful Academy painters were a powerful element in imaginative response to the fictions of the day; they created instantly identifiable stereotypes which could then be inserted by novel-readers' imaginations between the pages they turned.

Miss Yonge, however, did not wish to evoke fictional stereotypes of this kind; indeed, she distrusted them as being often productive of self-deception. To explore her treatment of such stereotypes, one might begin by citing another favourite image, R. B. Martineau's *The Last Chapter*, which portrays a girl kneeling by a grate to catch the fire-light on the book which is absorbing her. She might stand for Dolores Mohun in *The Two Sides of the Shield*, who sits on the floor to read *Clare, or No Home*, a sensational story about a persecuted golden-haired heiress, which Miss Yonge describes with gleeful mockery.

> Her golden hair was cut short by her wicked aunt, because it outshone her cousin's sandy locks. There was reason to think that a tress of this same golden hair would lead to her recognition by some grandfather of unknown magnificence, as exactly like that of his long-lost Claribel, and this might result in her assuming splendours that would annihilate the aunt. (*TSS* 00)

Dolores herself, whose mother is dead and who has been left in the care of an aunt, chooses to regard herself as persecuted and misunderstood though she is really treated with much imaginative sympathy by the aunt, Lady Merrifield, who confides to a friend that she has found among Dolores's books

> no less than four stories based on the cruelty and injustice suffered by orphans from their aunts. The wicked stepmothers are gone out, and the barbarous aunts are come in. It is the stock subject. I really think it is cruel, considering that there are many children who have to be adopted into uncles' families, to add to their distress and terror, by raising this prejudice. (*TSS* 356–7)

Was Miss Yonge thinking of Mrs Reed and her cruelty to her niece, the child Jane Eyre? The first two chapters of Charlotte Brontë's novel, with the vivid terrors of the Red Room where the child Jane is locked up, might well make any orphaned girl suspicious of all aunts as barbarous and unjust. It was a dangerous stereotype which Miss Yonge set out to break.

The best way to highlight this mission of hers is to analyse in some detail one novel of hers which exposes the falsity of no less than three popular stereotypes enshrined in novels and paintings of her time. The novel, *Hopes and Fears*, was published in 1860, and its basic theme is a warning against inordinate affection, the setting up of human idols. Unlike most of her novels, which tend to plunge immediately into dialogue on the opening page, it starts with a long description of two houses, a Jacobean house in the City of London and a half- timbered country mansion, and with a detailed picture of the landscape round the latter, a prospect of autumnal woods and fields very rare in her works, which in general do not have much sense of place outdoors. Here it serves a structural purpose, a prophetic glimpse of the life of the book's heroine, Honora Charlecote who (as Miss Yonge recalls in the last chapter of the book) is to go through a youthful spring-time nipped by the frost of disappointment, summer storms of twenty years of enthusiasms and disillusions, but after the autumn of her life seems to have set in, is to reach a late Indian summer of calm bright lingering farewell.

The opening chapters, however, are not well managed; the events of twelve years – in which Honora Charlecote is proposed to by her cousin Humphrey but is already unofficially engaged to Owen Sandbrook, who then goes to Canada as a missionary, marries another woman, comes back to a comfortable parish in England, loses his wife and one of his three children, confides the other two to Honora's care, and then dies abroad – are all summarized in paragraphs apt to start with 'Years passed on' or 'Seven years more'. Miss Yonge was not good at time-shift techniques, she handled the transitions between contemporary reporting and flashbacks rather awkwardly. But once Honora adopts the children Lucilla and young Owen Sandbrook, the narrative takes off, and there are no later flaggings. The core of the story which follows is her hopes and fears about the development of the two orphans as they grow up into personalities unforeseen by her in her efforts to form and educate them.

Here we encounter the first of the stereotypes which she exposes in this novel. The icon which might be chosen to represent this stereotype could be Millais's *Bubbles*, that all-pervading image which became a soap advertisement, or perhaps James Sant's *The Infant Samuel*, the much-reproduced image of a huge-eyed little boy having a spiritual revelation. The saintly child, very often on his death-bed, was a cherished icon, displayed not only by Evangelical tract-writers but also by such admirable authors as Mrs Gaskell and Mrs Ewing, and most famously by Dickens with Paul Dombey. Almost as many tears were shed over Paul Dombey as over Little Nell, as Miss Yonge recognized when she referred in *The Heir of Redclyffe* to 'the part of *Dombey* that hurts women's feelings most . . . the part about little Paul', over which Amy Edmondstone is found weeping in the greenhouse (*HR* 23). Miss Yonge herself had created a rather insufferably saintly little boy, Johnny Martindale, in an earlier novel, *Heartsease*, but Johnny is saved from utter priggishness by being a physical coward, frightened of other children and terrified of cows, and though sickly, he lives to grow up. Miss Yonge did not go in for pious death-beds for children in her novels, indeed was inclined to mock other novelists such as Mrs Sherwood who made much of them. Considering the size of Miss Yonge's many fictional large families, and the child mortality rates in Victorian real life, there are surprisingly few children's deaths in her novels, and where they do happen – as with the retarded Theodore in *The Pillars of the House*, drowned in a boating accident – there are no edifying death-bed speeches.

In *Hopes and Fears* she set out to undermine the stereotype of the holy child, the Infant Samuel, whose infantile piety is a matter of sentimental enthusiasm not grounded on solid principle. Honora Charlecote spoils her adopted son Owen who, 'with his innocent earnestness, and the spiritual light in his eyes', will, she believes, fulfil all her dreams of a saintly hero, which his father had disappointed. At the age of four his touching sayings about his parents being among the angels in heaven, his wish to become a clergyman like his father, his childish sweetness, convince her that he needs no discipline because he never does anything wrong. As he grows up he continues to be regarded as an 'angelic little mortal', taught entirely by Honora till he goes to a public school, 'like a spirited horse in a leash of silk. Strong, fearless and manly, he was still perfectly amenable to her, and had never shown any impatience of her rule', but was still full of pious observance and apparently keen to become a clergyman. Honora considers him perfect, but there have already been signs that, encouraged by flattering servants, he is counting on inheriting her estate when she dies, and a few years later, when he is a tall young man, Honora is shattered by the revelations that he has consistently lied to her, has eloped with a pretty village schoolmistress, and has raised a post-orbit on Honora's estate. She has to acknowledge that

> Fond affection had led her to put herself into a position to which Providence did not call her, and to which she was, therefore, unequal. Fond affection had blinded her eyes, and fostered in its object the very faults most hateful to her. (*HF* 310)

The dangers of being deluded by the holy child stereotype have been convincingly demonstrated. Long afterwards Honora admits

> Ah! once I spurned, and afterwards grieved over, the saying that very religious little boys either die or belie their promise. (*HF* 636)

But she has learnt to accept Owen as he really is, not as she had blindly believed him to be, to continue to love him while leaving her estate away from him to someone with a better claim who will make better use of it.

Though the character and fortunes of Owen Sandbrook and his sister Lucilla are the main thread of *Hopes and Fears*, the novel has a complex texture of the interlocking developments in four connected family groups, the Charlecotes, the Sandbrooks, the Charterises and the Fulmorts, and Miss Yonge weaves these different strands into her pattern with skill and agility. Honora Charlecote is always in the frame, sometimes as the central figure, sometimes in the middle distance moving from group to group, sometimes just an observer in the background. The focus shifts from group to group; sometimes for several consecutive chapters we are entirely in the Fulmort mansion, Beauchamp, inhabited by a gin-distiller father, an almost mentally deficient heiress mother, an elder son and daughters who are selfish and worldly, and then a son and daughter, Robert and Phoebe, who come under Honora's influence and gain from her the principled piety which she failed to impart to Owen Sandbrook, and who become the secondary juvenile leads of the novel. But much the most interesting inhabitant of Beauchamp is not a member of the Fulmort family, but the governess Miss Fennimore, and in her the reader confronts another powerfully exploded stereotype.

The idea of a Victorian governess is epitomized by a brilliantly successful and popular icon, Richard Redgrave's painting *The Young Governess*, also known as *The Poor Teacher*. Thackeray, as art critic for *Fraser's Magazine*, wrote an emotional description of the young woman in the picture in her black dress, sitting desolately in her schoolroom with her meagre supper, a slice of bread and butter, on the table beside her; she has left it untouched because of the black-edged letter from home which she has just been reading and which rests on her knee. With a sob in his throat Thackeray wrote 'There she sits, poor dear! – the piano is open beside her and (oh, harrowing thought!) "Home, Sweet Home" is open in the music book'.

Prints of the picture were widely circulated, and its central position in Victorian literary consciousness is shown by Jean Ingelow's story 'Dr Deane's Governess' (mentioned with approval by Miss Yonge in *Womankind*) in which, referring to the picture as though everyone knew of it, Jean Ingelow describes a farmer's daughter, a healthy well-treated girl, who has seen the Redgrave print and has also brooded over a novel in which a persecuted governess marries a baronet. Thereafter the girl is always carefully arranging herself in the forlorn pose of Redgrave's governess, trying to look dejected and pathetic, and allowing it to be assumed that she is a high-born heroine in painfully reduced circumstances.

In fact, if the great mass of Victorian fiction were to be accepted as a guide, there would be no need to feel sorry for Redgrave's governess; she would soon make a prosperous marriage above her station into her employers' family, whether she was a Jane Eyre or a Becky Sharp. She is a governess by situation, not by vocation; her prime destiny is matrimony, or at any rate romantic love. As a device of plot, the governess in Victorian novels took the place of an orphan in a ruined castle in the Gothic ones, and was only to relinquish her Cinderella throne in the twentieth century to the typist and the hospital nurse. Her position made her a perfect focus for attracting the reader's attention and sympathy. She could be bullied by her pupils, scorned and exploited by their mother and her friends, pestered by the attentions of the loutish son of the house. Like Dickens's Ruth Pinch, and Harriet Martineau's Maria Young in *Deerbrook*, she could provoke resentment and ill-treatment from her vulgar employers by her very refinement. If, like George Eliot's Maggie Tulliver and Mrs Gaskell's Ruth, she had been helped to a governess's job by a compassionate clergyman, she could be cruelly driven out of it again by malicious tongues. Whether she was destined to an illustrious marriage or a saintly death-bed, she was an invaluable plot-making nexus for virtually every Victorian novelist, though few of them went quite as far as Mrs Henry Wood, whose heroine Lady Isabel, after eloping with a lover and being disfigured in a railway accident, returned in disguise as a governess to her own children.

Miss Yonge will have none of this. Her governesses – and her novels are full of them – are professional women doing a job; few of them get married, hardly any of them are ill-treated. She despised the 'pathetic governess style', with its pernicious influence on the day-dreams of real-life governesses.

> Insolence to a governess is an old stock complaint. In real life, I never heard of it from anyone by birth and breeding a lady (WK 34)

she said roundly. She herself had never either had, or been, a governess; she was educated entirely at home, by her parents and visiting masters. Anne Brontë, who had herself been a governess, may be thought to have depicted more of the realities of exploited governess life in her largely autobiographical *Agnes Grey*, but she hardly exhibits her heroine as a professional teacher. Miss Yonge regarded governesses as professionals like lawyers and doctors, and it is that aspect of governess life, not the pathos and exploitation of Redgrave's icon, that she explores in her novels.

The redoubtable Miss Fennimore in *Hopes and Fears* is a highly paid expert, given a free hand by her pupils' parents, and wielding a powerful influence in the household. She is a forty-two-year-old scholar at the height of her powers, a brilliant systematic unrelenting teacher, to whom the intellectual activity involved is her highest sport and pleasure. She concentrated on teaching girls from fifteen to eighteen, and had virtually killed one former pupil, acute in mind but frail in body, by over-working and over-stimulating her. But she could adapt her methods to her pupils; the moderately able but thorough and conscientious Phoebe Fulmort was given just the systematic cramming that exercised her mind to the full, while her mentally deficient sister Maria was patiently trained within the narrow limits of her powers. (Maria perhaps had Down's syndrome; Miss Yonge would not have known the name of the disease, but she described its symptoms with a clinical perspicacity worthy of her medical ancestors, who included the seventeenth-century Dr James Yonge of Plymouth famous for his expertise at trepanning). Today a woman like Miss Fennimore would be the star tutor of a prestigious crammers establishment, who would get the most unpromising pupils through their A levels. She makes a startling and convincing contrast to the conventional governess of Victorian fiction. Whereas some of Miss Yonge's contemporaries, like Anna Jameson, thought the governess/employer situation unworkably difficult, and declared that 'A woman who knows anything of the world would, if the choice were left to her, be anything in the world rather than a governess',[1] Miss Yonge wanted to convince her readers (many of whom may have been, or become, governesses themselves) that with good will on both sides, the relationship could be made to work. There is an admirable description in *The Daisy Chain* of the Mays' governess Miss Bracy, who is pleasing and well-qualified but terribly touchy; her feelings are hurt by the mildest criticism, even by quite imaginary slights, and she makes Ethel May's life a continual irritation both by her demonstrative affection and by her easily wounded feelings. Dr May's ability both to sympathize with Miss Bracy's morbid sensitivity in her dependent situation, and to give her bracing advice, does in the end stop Miss Bracy from brooding over fancied slights, and even enables her to pass on this more sensible frame of mind to a friend, another governess whose employers are less considerate than the Mays.

This depth of texture conferred on quite minor characters in Miss Yonge's novels gives them a richness which is often only fully enjoyed on a second or third reading. She hardly ever, at least in the novels of her maturity, leaves even her peripheral characters flat and two-dimensional. *Hopes and Fears* is full of rounded portraits of minor characters, and one of these provides the third instance of a fictional stereotype rejected.

No icon for this third stereotype comes to mind, but it is easy to imagine such a picture. It would probably be by John Collier, and it would show a middle-aged man, with signs of past dissipation on his haggard but tranquil face, sunk back in a fireside chair; leaning over his shoulder would be his smiling little wife, pointing out a text in the Bible open on his knee. The title would be 'Saved by the Love of a Good Woman'. There is no lack of fictional parallels, such as Laura Pendennis, Mary Garth in *Middlemarch*, David Copperfield's appalling Agnes, forever pointing upward. Miss Yonge herself produced an instance of this stereotype in the early *Heartsease*, whose heroine Violet Martindale becomes the guiding light not only of her selfish gambling husband but of his whole family. But in *Hopes and Fears* Miss Yonge was brave and honest enough to admit that the formula might not always work.

Mervyn, eldest of the Fulmort family, fell in love as a young man with the homely serious Cecily Raymond, but was rejected, in spite of her love for him, because her family considered he had sowed too many wild oats to be a safe choice. The rejection, which the wealthy young squire had not in the least expected, drove him to further dissipation. When he has partly reformed, they are finally allowed to marry, but the result is not a success.

> Strict, scrupulous, and deeply devout, the clergyman's daughter suffered at every deviation from the practices of the Parsonage, made her stand in the wrong places, and while conscientiously and painfully fretting Mervyn about petty details, would be unknowingly carried over far greater stumbling-blocks. In her ignorance she would be distressed at habits which were comparatively innocent, and then fear to put forth her influence at the right moment. There was hearty affection on either side, and Mervyn was exceedingly improved, but more than once Phoebe saw in poor Cecily's harassed, puzzled, wistful face, and heard in her faltering remonstrances, what it was to have loved and married without perfect esteem and trust. (*HF* 616)

That is a very acute portrait of a marriage; Miss Yonge continually surprises by such unexpected insights.

She was convinced that fiction – even well-meaning fiction that contained nothing obviously shocking or depraved – could exercise a bad influence. It could promote self-deception and soft-centred enthusiasms, could make easy solutions and short cuts seem possible, could raise fanciful expectations. By subtle and ingenious strategies she set herself to dismantle dangerous stereotypes which might corrupt the honesty of readers' responses, and dissipate their energies in idle dreams.

4

Historical Imagination

Miss Yonge educated herself by her very wide range of reading. She never went to school. Her father taught her mathematics and Latin, she had visiting masters for French, Spanish and Italian, but the greater part of her schoolroom hours were spent in reading on her own, though the books were chosen by her parents. Before she was five, she was already spending an hour a day on reading, and having history lessons once a week. As a teenager she had to read twenty pages a day of some history book; when that not unwelcome task was over, her reward was to be allowed to read a chapter of a novel by Walter Scott, and then whatever she liked among books of travel, Bowdlerized Shakespeare, translations of Greek tragedies. Her refreshment from solid reading was more solid reading. With Keble she read Dante, Spenser, Wordsworth, Manzoni. By the time she was grown up she had read all the great English poets and many other classics of English literature, including Jane Austen's novels, to which she was devoted. The greatest influence on her was that of Walter Scott, of whom, as man and as author, she was a deeply admiring disciple. Her own books are pervaded by quotations from Scott's novels, and still more from his poetry, some of the quotations oblique enough not to be readily intelligible to a modern reader, but Miss Yonge assumed as a matter of course that all her readers would know their Scott well enough to be able to pick up such references. 'You can hardly be called a well-educated person if you do not know them' says a father to a daughter forbidden by a stern older sister to read Scott's novels (*SC* 24). She often illustrated her own characters' tendencies by describing their reaction to Scott's novels, in *The Trial, The Pillars of the House, Magnum Bonum*; did they give themselves away by weeping over Marmion, making fun of the Maid of Lorn, adoring Sir Kenneth of the Leopard?

Most of Miss Yonge's characters are great readers; many conversations in her novels are discussions of other writers' books – not a common feature of Victorian fiction; who in the novels of Dickens ever reads a book, except Silas Wegg, not exactly a devotee of literature?

Miss Yonge did not only read classics of the past, she read the novels of her great contemporaries, Dickens, Thackeray, Trollope, the Brontës, George Eliot, Mrs Gaskell, though she never met any of them; she had, and wanted, no access to the literary circles of her day. Some of her comments on the work of her contemporaries are crass enough; she considered the Brontës 'coarse', Carlyle 'a humbug', George Eliot's ideals 'absurd' and her 'defiance of all moral and religious principles' deplorable (ER 80, 155–6, CC 340). She rated Keble's verse in *The Christian Year* so highly as to suggest that she had little ear for poetry. Her snap judgments on her contemporaries' writing were more moral than aesthetic; if some work by Byron or by George Eliot attracted her reluctant admiration, she was all the more ready to put it on the index – its very power over the reader made its evil propensities more dangerous. Shelley and Dumas are both used in her novels as illustrations of the fatal influence of potent but unprincipled literature. *The Monthly Packet* always included a 'Hints on Reading' section, and late in her life she published an advice manual, *What Books To Lend And What To Give*, intended chiefly for the guidance of school librarians, which included late-nineteenth-century writers like Robert Louis Stevenson and Rider Haggard, as well as a host of earlier writers from Bunyan to Kingsley and Lewis Carroll, selections intended mainly for every age of working-class readers from children under eight to their fathers. She showed a reasonable understanding of what might bore or alienate the exhausted domestic servants or working men who only wanted recreation, not improvement, from their reading. Her thorough study of reader reactions always modified her expectations of how much could be done by role models, and is best shown in her only considerable piece of literary criticism, the admirable series of articles on 'Children's Literature of the Last Century' published in *Macmillan's Magazine* in 1869, and much quoted in recent histories of children's fiction. Kathleen Tillotson, in 'Charlotte Yonge as a Critic of Literature' (B and L 56–7) is reminded of Dr Johnson and Matthew Arnold when rating Miss Yonge's critical powers, and suggests that the total of her essays on literature, in articles, reviews, prefaces and critical notes, could make up two large volumes if collected. It would at least show some of the enormous scope of her reading.

Her thorough and lifelong research in printed historical sources, in French, German and Latin as well as English, is her real claim to scholarly status. Her theological works – *Conversations on the Catechism, Musings on 'The Christian Year', Reasons Why I Am A Catholic And Not A Roman Catholic* – are densely textured with doctrines and quotations from the Early Fathers and ecclesiastical history. Readers often asked her for 'pièces justificatives', her authorities for the abundant detail and incident of her historical novels and tales, and she began to supply these in prefaces, recording astonishingly wide lists of sources in histories, biographies, topographical works. Historical research was a much-enjoyed refreshment in her writing life, and she regarded it as 'the best school for one's mind or for fiction. If I write nothing but fiction for some time I begin to get stupid, and to feel rather as if it had been a long meal of sweets; then history is a rest, for research or narration brings a different part of the mind into play' (GB 116). She displayed real serendipity in picking out vivid incidents from a mass of material. Her power of selecting significant detail from a complicated but thoroughly studied background is shown in such sketches as the story of 'The Five Sisters of Noailles' (Madame de Lafayette and her sisters) during the French Revolution and the Napoleonic Wars. She deliberately chose to present history through the personal angle, through lives of individuals, thereby catching the attention of whole generations of young readers whom she inoculated with a love of history, as well as proposing role models to them. Her aid as a teacher of history was sought by such academics as E. A. Freeman and J. R. Green, who respected her historical knowledge sufficiently to ask for her cooperation over history textbook series.

By today's standards she would not be recognized as a historian in the full sense, because she rarely examined original unprinted documents (she did do some research of this kind at Hatfield when she was writing *Unknown to History*, but that was exceptional), and only sometimes – as when she contrived a tour of inspection of Portland Prison when she was writing *The Trial* – verified the scenes and institutions which she so freely described in her novels.

Nevertheless she had the quality of a true historian. Even in her childhood she had begun to train her mind in historical method and imagination. One of the Moberly family described how, as a shrill-voiced twelve-year-old, shy and bored by formal calls, Miss Yonge would relieve the tedium of the callers' conversation by imagining that they were in another period of history and were discussing the prospect of invasion by the Spanish Armada.[1] She had the kind of historical imagination which enabled her to empathize with the cultural attitudes and predispositions of a period, as well as to reproduce its external trappings. Thus in *Love and Life* she is able convincingly to list the textbooks from which a six-year-old boy would learn in the reign of George II, and the French books that his elder sisters are likely to have read. Even in a late tired work like *The Pilgrimage of the Ben Beriah*, an unsuccessful attempt, with stock characters and sagging narrative, to bring the grand landscape of the Exodus closer to young readers by adding fictional figures to the foreground, she shows an unexpected and imaginative conception of the confusion between the religion of the God of Israel and the pagan worship of the gods of Egypt which simple Israelitish women felt after generations of bondage in Egypt.

She is often, and with some justification, accused of distorting historical facts in her novels to reinforce some moral message, of imbuing everyone – from slaves in Roman Gaul to medieval chiefs in the Scottish Highlands – with the pious sentiments of a nineteenth-century Tractarian gentleman. She would have used in her defence against such a charge the claim – defined by C. S. Lewis as The Fallacy of the Unchanging Human Heart – that 'If times differ, human and national character vary but little; and thus, in looking back at former times, we are by turns startled by what is curiously like, and curiously unlike, our own sayings and doings', as she put it in one of the prefaces to her historical novels in which she constantly examined the contrast between historical accuracy and authorial imperatives (LL vol 1, p. i). In theory, she held that earlier historical novelists, even the revered Walter Scott, were not justified in the extent to which they carved history to suit the purposes of their story, and that such practices were no longer acceptable. In practice, she did the same thing herself, not only to reinforce moral messages but to suit her literary ends; her prefaces, though apologetic about this, confess the inability of the novelist to resist an anachronism which enhances the story, the need to rearrange and curtail historical facts to grip the reader's attention. She even admitted that her historical tales were 'intended to describe what might have been, rather than what actually was', and such was her honesty that she could say that non-fictional abridgements of adult history were better than 'tons of babyish "Stories from Froissart", "Stories of Cavaliers and Roundheads" etc made into fictional pap' (CLLC 455). Once again she appears to be sawing off the branch on which she is sitting.

Whatever her own qualms about writing them, the best of her historical tales – *The Little Duke, The Chaplet of Pearls, The Dove in the Eagle's Nest* – have continued to captivate readers by their sheer narrative excitement. She knew very well what she was doing; with her eye constantly on readership reactions, she recognized that the attention of the ordinary reader 'has learnt to feed upon character and incident, and to require that the latter should be effective and exciting. Is it not reasonable to seek for this in the days when such things were not infrequent, and did not imply exceptional wickedness or misfortune in those engaged in them?' (*CP* pp. vii–viii). In her family chronicles of her own time, she was to some extent restricted by her observation of the real life around her; in her historical novels her imagination, over which history had always had an exceptional power, as she acknowledged, ran more freely, including elements of fantasy and romance which have always made this side of her work appeal to a slightly different readership from the devotees of her contemporary family chronicles. The critical event in *The Dove in the Eagle's Nest* originated in a dream Miss Yonge had after reading a history of Germany, and it is arguable that her subconscious was given a more free rein in her historical romances than in her other novels. But she kept her objective in writing this – or any other – type of book steadily in mind. 'The dream that has been pleasant to dream may be pleasant to listen to . . . this style of composition does tend to fix young people's interest and attention on the scenes it treats of, and to vivify the characters it describes, and if this sketch at all prepares young people's minds to look with sympathy and appreciation on any of the great characters of our early annals, it will have done at least one work' (*PP* p. viii).

The historical novels and stories were written primarily for young readers, but as Henry James said of *The Heir of Redclyffe,* they belong to the class of books which grown women can read to children without either being bored (KT 39). They are written for children in a simple and straightforward but not 'told-to-the-children' style. She did not believe in making stories too easily accessible for readers of any age. Children should be encouraged to 'stretch up to books above them', even if they did not understand every word; if they were held by the story, they would assimilate unfamiliar words and facts (CLLC 456).

Her stories in this genre sometimes had a real historical figure – Mary Queen of Scots, the Emperor Maximilian, King Henry V – as a central figure, but their normal pattern, based on her model Walter Scott, is to include real-life characters in the middle distance, the foreground being occupied by imaginary contemporaries of theirs. She did not restrict herself to any special period; her full-length romances range through almost every century of European history from the ninth to the eighteenth. Nor did she concentrate on British, or even European, localities; there are tales set in Ancient Egypt and Palestine as well as Germany, France, Scotland. Her very wide reading, and her prodigious memory for the smallest facts in the histories she read, enabled her to picture customs and living conditions of different periods – dress, diet, architecture, travel, rituals and ceremonies, superstitions, allegiances, codes of manners – in convincing and vivid detail.

Her historical output was not restricted to fiction. All through her writing career she dashed off volume after volume of historical sketches, perhaps modelled on Plutarch, of famous men and women and heroic deeds, of summaries of historic periods: *Cameos from History* (nine volumes), *Landmarks of History, Book of Worthies, Biographies of Good Women, Aunt Charlotte's Stories of American, Bible, English, French, German, Greek, Roman History, Kings of England*, and many more. Some were originally contributed to *The Monthly Packet*, some were textbooks and primers for school-children of various ages. She also published a number of translations of French memoirs and history. Her output was prodigious, and inevitably uneven in quality and interest, but her aim of enlivening dull history for young readers by singling out striking events and heroic characters to illuminate their historical surroundings was often achieved. Her many stories of the courageous deeds of biblical, classical and historical 'worthies' appealed to the same readers who thrilled to Macaulay's *Lays of*

Ancient Rome, though neither author would have relishéd the comparison. The quality which most attracted her was courage, not mere brute boldness, but disciplined, steadfast chivalrous courage, and in portraying it she showed a toughness which often surprises. She was not squeamish. She shared with Keble a passion for reading and talking about battles. War to her was glorious; she might have made a brilliant and thorough military historian. She had no qualms about envisaging or describing violent events. In a late story, *Founded on Paper*, a drunken and desperate workman shoots his wife, tries to drown his small children, and then kills himself, and these events are described, not with gusto, but with open-eyed realism. The most remarkable instance of this unsqueamish toughness is her *Book of Golden Deeds*. This used for half a century or so to be one of the most often bestowed school prizes. Modern critics who label it sweet and soothing can hardly have read it.[2] A careful parent today would be more likely to deplore its choice as a school prize because it is too bloodthirsty and frightening, not because it is too emollient, for child readers. In it Miss Yonge describes tortures, wounds, murders and massacres, not with relish, but unsparingly, as the framework of her heroes' actions. Quite a strong stomach is needed to read the account of the prolonged agonies of Rudolf von der Wart, the story of the brave and faithful but far from exemplary Russian soldier among the Chechens, the examples of Manlius Torquatus and Alonso Perez de Guzman in allowing their own sons to be executed for the sake of patriotic duty. The 'Golden Deeds' do include rescues from, and self-sacrifice in, fires, plagues, snow-storms, shipwrecks, and some achievements of saints like Geneviève or Vincent de Paul, some records of faithful servants, but the great majority of the deeds take place in the context of battles, mob violence, assassinations and insurrections. If anxious parents today might want to avert such horrors from their children, most child watchers of Superman-type videos would enjoy *A Book of Golden Deeds* very much.

Though she wrote such quantities of short biographical sketches, Miss Yonge only produced one full-length biography, her *Life of John Coleridge Patteson, Missionary Bishop of the Melanesian Islands*. She found the task, undertaken at the request of the martyred bishop's sisters, a daunting one, and her definition of her method in writing it suggests that in dealing with a contemporary she felt an obligation to be objective which did not hamper her sketches of past history. 'I think I have represented fairly, for I have done my best faithfully to select passages giving his mind even where it does not coincide completely with my own opinions; being quite convinced that not only should a biographer never attempt either to twist or conceal the sentiments of the subject, but that either to apologise for, or as it were to argue with them, is vain in both senses of the word' (*LBP* vol 1, pp. vi–vii). It is a creditably scholarly approach, but the result was a straight-forward and well-researched work, respectable but not enthralling. Keble once suggested that she should write a biography of King Henry VI, and it might have been interesting to see what she made of another saintly martyr, but she was best at conveying biographical facts in brief brilliant sketches, rather than in extended concentration on a single figure, and she herself acknowledged her unfitness for the task in her preface to the *Life of Bishop Patteson*.

Her only real claim to authority as a scholar rests on her *History of Christian Names*. Hers was the first serious attempt at tackling onomastics as an independent subject; it was her highly original idea to explore 'the capabilities of the subject of comparative nomenclature . . . as an illustration of language, national character, religion and taste' (*HCN* vol 1, p. 5). Her pioneering work has been described as 'a great deal better than anything that had gone before, and, indeed, than most of its successors . . . It has ever since remained the standard work on the subject in English, and practically the whole substance of later books has been based on it, their authors, sometimes openly and sometimes tacitly, using it as a quarry'.[3] The research which she did for this work was impressive. She had been 'collecting for years, from dictionaries, books of travel, histories and popular tales' (*HCN* vol 1, p. vii); she consulted works on Hebrew, Greek, Roman, Anglo-Saxon, German, Scandinavian, Celtic, Erse philology and nomenclature, the proceedings of such specialized bodies as the Ossianic Society, a whole wide-ranging network of sources from Welsh dictionaries to French hagiologies, from biblical studies to the *Nibelungenlied*. She traced the evolution and historical context of first names, a scholarly approach which she had worked out for herself with no formal academic training and no easy access to learned libraries. She did, however, manage to buy or borrow a very wide range of learned books and periodicals, and to correspond with Norwegian, Welsh and other authorities. The application of historical methods to linguistic studies was an almost unknown discipline in her day, and though more recent research has invalidated some of her etymology, her book remains a valuable compendium of facts, anecdotes and comparative culture studies.

It also provided her with some very unusual Christian names – Metelill, Uchtred, Annora, Wilmet, Ermine – for characters in her novels, and an amusing eighteenth-century disguise, in her *Love and Life*, patterned on the story of Cupid and Psyche, for her characters, Psyche becoming the butterfly equivalent Aurelia, Cupid masked as Amyas Belamour, Vulcan as Mr Wayland, and so on. She used mythological and folklore frameworks for several novels such as *My Young Alcides, A Modern Telemachus* and *A Reputed Changeling*. It has even been suggested that *The Heir of Redclyffe* has an allegorical pattern of Spring and the Sun (Guy) in conflict with Winter and Darkness (Philip) (SD 30–7) or that Guy represents Parsifal, the Holy Fool. Miss Yonge's formidable knowledge of classical and English myths and legends was analysed in *Folklore in the Works of Charlotte Yonge* by the folklorist authority Katharine Briggs, who commends her as a recorder of surviving superstitions and customs in the countryside of her own day.

She recalled some of these in the charming *An Old Woman's Outlook in a Hampshire Village*, a month-by-month record of botanical and ornithological observations almost worthy to be compared with Gilbert White's annals of another Hampshire village a few miles away, a hundred years earlier. She was an experienced botanist, who kept records and dried specimens of wild flowers, and a conchologist whose collection of shells was thought worthy of acceptance by Winchester College as a bequest. Children in her stories keep silk-worms, hunt for fossils, make butterfly collections; she had a passion for natural history rather than for English landscape, which plays no great part in her novels. Her sense of place is strongest for imagined domestic interiors, which she often lovingly described, and even illustrated by plans. It is curious that she, a lifelong village inhabitant, was better at portraying townscapes – whether seaside resorts or city slums – than the woods and fields which she knew so well. She did not think that the novelist was bound only to locate his characters in places known to his own experience. 'It is in the power of imagination to call up before it places unseen but described, so as to picture them vividly in words to other auditors' she asserted, quoting Bulwer-Lytton (*MCY* 13, 164), and although her own overseas excursions were only to Ireland and France, she had no qualms about locating scenes and whole sections of her novels in distant parts of the world – the USA, Polynesia, Sicily, Panama. She gave vivid pictures of the mountains and silver mines of Peru, the bougainvillaea and orange blossom of a Moorish courtyard in Algeria, the deserts and wells of Sinai and Palestine. One whole novel, *New Ground*, about missionaries in South Africa, contains detailed descriptions of African birds, insects and flowers, which she must have culled from the missionaries' reports which were a much-appreciated element in her very wide reading.

The charm of *An Old Woman's Outlook* is not in middle-distance landscape descriptions, but in close-up views of wild flowers, birds' nests, spiders' webs, and in the incidental side-lights it casts on village sayings, habits, superstitions, and how these changed during her long life in one place. The value of Miss Yonge's books as a barometer of social change is an important aspect of her work, and of her strong perception of the historical process, which will be considered in the next chapter.

5

Social Change: Nostalgia and Acceptance

Miss Yonge's novels and short stories of working-class life are now little known, but they are important from the point of view of social history, and include some of her best writing of the 1880s and 1890s, a period in her career of authorship when she is generally considered to have lost her grip. The series of stories about village children are the cream of the copious flow of textbooks, teaching manuals, anthologies, abridgements, which she poured out as a result of her own teaching experience in village schools. She taught the children of Otterbourne in the Church school there all her life, starting at the age of seven and continuing to the year of her death nearly seventy years later. By all accounts she was a brilliant teacher, whose lessons were remembered even in old age by her former pupils. All her normal shyness and awkwardness with the working-class villagers disappeared completely when she was actually teaching. She had the gift of devising varied and imaginative techniques to hold attention and stimulate interest. Hours of her busy life were spared to the preparation of lessons for her village pupils; she kept records of their answers, and discussed them with like-minded friends. The insight into children's minds which she gained by this teaching gave her the material for her village stories.

Some of her series on the imaginary Langley School and its pupils have been republished recently as *Village Children* with an introduction by Gillian Avery, but most have become all but inaccessible. Unlike her family chronicle novels, which were aimed at a readership of middle-class young girls, her village stories were for, as well as about, working-class children, and were often given as school prizes. A typical example, *The Treasures in the Marshes*, has an entirely working-class cast of gardeners, farm-hands, washerwomen and parlourmaids, and their living conditions, diet, clothes and attitudes to their employers and the police are knowledgeably described; the hardships of the rural poor are not disguised. The moral – that honesty is the best policy – is not too heavily emphasized. The good do prosper in the end, while the wicked suffer and finally repent; but the virtuous characters are often unimaginative and awkward, and some of the sinners are warm-hearted and spontaneous. The story has a vivid framework of weather and wild life.

Such sympathetic understanding of the lives of the poor might not have been expected from a natural unquestioning Tory like Miss Yonge. She saw no need for radical reform of the status quo of class division and financial inequality. In this as in all else a Tractarian, she understood her duty to her neighbours to be the alleviation of individual suffering and deprivation, not the reorganization of society as a whole. Her father and Keble had immovably moulded her allegiance to the political party which alone, they believed, could safeguard the country's religion. 'Do not Liberals show themselves to be the Church's natural enemies?' she anxiously queried.[1] But except in relation to the Church, she was not much interested in politics, or at all in economics. Some critics have suggested that she was locked into nostalgia for an imaginary golden age of the past (BD 30), in which she located her vision of the ideal society. It is true that, like George Eliot with *Middlemarch*, Charlotte Brontë with *Shirley*, Thackeray with *Vanity Fair*, she set several of her novels in the world of her childhood, half a century earlier than the time of writing. *Chantry House* is set in the 1820s and 1830s, the period of agricultural riots. She seems to have been fascinated by memories of the hardship and unrest, the rick-burning and marauding of 'Jack Swing'. She and her parents were in Devonshire when the rioters threatened Hampshire landowners, but the misery of the time was brought close to her when her nurse's two brothers were sentenced to be hanged for their part in the riots. The events of those years caught her historic interest, but hardly her nostalgia. She was well aware of the rural wretchedness of the period, as she showed with even-handed objectivity in another very interesting picture of the 1820s, *The Carbonels*, in which the central characters are not the gentry – who play an important but secondary role in the story – but the working-class villagers in a farming community. She is surprisingly un-mealy-mouthed about the squalor, wife-beating, male and female drunkenness, theft and lies of some of the villagers, and their immovable prejudices and suspicion of the motives of upper-class do-gooders; but she is equally critical of selfish irresponsible landowners who exploit their half-starved workers and abuse them as ungrateful and good-for-nothing, and criticize any attempt to improve their lot as a waste of time. She draws no general sociological conclusions from the state of affairs she describes. In her view the poor should be helped, but will be always with us; the alternatives are good or bad landowner employers, not maintaining or abolishing landowning altogether. What makes this novel still worth reading is not her reactionary political stance but her close observation of the appearance, speech and manners of the farm workers. She can understand, even sympathize with, their class solidarity which makes even the best of them, grateful as they are to a benevolent employer, reluctant to betray a plot to attack him and his farm. It was necessary, she concedes, to 'make allowances for the bewilderment of slow minds, for sheer cowardice, and for the instinct of going along with one's own class of people'. She could even understand and respect the idealism motivating some of the rick-burners. 'There were hot spirits abroad, who knew that much was amiss in many points, and who burned to set them right', though she maintained that such wrongs would be righted gradually and peacefully if the workers would only be patient (*TC* pp. cxxv, 245). A sequel to *The Carbonels, Founded on Paper*, portrayed the same rural community two generations later, between Queen Victoria's two Jubilees, when a railway station and factories have transformed the scene; there is less dire poverty, more schooling, more social mobility.

It is these objective records of rural conditions and change that make Miss Yonge valuable as a social historian. She did not welcome change, but she observed it with a keen eye for detail which makes her a reliable witness to social developments in England between the 1820s and the 1890s. Her novels are a mine of information about the growth of towns, the effects of mechanization, rising levels of wages, the gradual breakdown of class barriers, changes in mourning and funeral customs, developments in health care and sanitation. Epidemics as a result of bad sewage provide turning-points in several of her novels, in *The Trial*, *The Young Stepmother*, *The Three Brides*. The changing face of the English countruside during the century is illustrated in the family chronicles by her pictures of such imaginary localities as Cocksmoor and Rockquay. Cocksmoor starts, in *The Daisy Chain*, as a collection of miserable mud huts round a slate quarry on a boggy moor. The efforts of the May family endow it first with a school, then with a church; and by the end of the novel the hamlet itself already shows signs of improvement in mended windows and railings and productive gardens. Forty years later, in *The Long Vacation*, it has become an industrial suburb of the nearby town of Market Stoneborough, and has a paper mill and two churches. Rockquay, originally a fishing village, first appears in *Beechcroft at Rockstone* as a fashionable seaside resort with handsome crescents and villas, but with unspoilt Devonshire combes and rocky streams and copses full of primroses near at hand. By the end of the last family chronicle, *Modern Broods*, these exquisite valleys have been ravished by a railway driven through them.

Above all, Miss Yonge was interested in educational developments. She believed in, and made a considerable contribution to, primary education for all children, which she promoted not only through her own teaching at Otterbourne school and the textbooks and library lists which she produced for schools all over the country, but through the extraordinary impetus she gave to voluntary teaching by young ladies who read her novels and *The Monthly Packet*. 'Many a real Cocksmoor has been taken in hand under the influence of *The Daisy Chain*', as Ethel Romanes testified (ER 199). Such teaching filled what was in the first half of the century a real gap. But the essence of the voluntary work was in Miss Yonge's opinion that it was directed by the Church; whether actual Sunday school teaching of religious subjects, or weekday teaching of history, arithmetic, literature, it was inspired and guided by Church doctrine and practice. She dreaded, and in her novels frequently inveighed against, 'godless education', and watched with dismay the appearance of Board schools, certificated teachers and inspectors, the secularization of education which culminated in the Act of 1870. Gradually, nevertheless, she began to accept the need for teachers to be qualified by training, for teenage girls to sit for public examinations, even eventually for the establishment of women's colleges at Oxford and Cambridge. At first she refused to lend support to the projects for their foundation, but two of her closest friends, Elizabeth Wordsworth and Anne Moberly, became Principals of Lady Margaret Hall and St Hugh's at Oxford, and she was won over; in her last family chronicle, *Modern Broods*, we actually encounter a heroine who is an Oxford undergraduate.

The fact that Miss Yonge did not like most of the changes she observed does not invalidate her as a witness, because she recognized the historical inevitability of change, and in her old age she achieved a puzzled but resigned acceptance of developments she at first deplored. She was 'an example of that typically English paradox, a progressive conservative, demanding not changelessness but continuity . . . Essentially incapable of progress herself, she yet admired and encouraged progress in others' (GB 122–3, 147). Her later novels include admired characters with elements of self-portrait like Felix Underwood in *The Pillars of the House*, Honora Charlecote in *Hopes and Fears*, Lilias Merrifield in *The Long Vacation*, who ruefully admit that their ideals are now considered old-fashioned by the younger generation. 'My enthusiasm', Lady Merrifield confesses to a friend of her own generation, 'was for chivalry, Christian chivalry, half symbolic. History was delightful to me for the search for true knights' but her more thoroughly educated children prove to her that 'the Cid was a ruffian, and the Black Prince not much better . . . Is it progress?'

'Well, I suppose it is, in a way' concedes her friend (*LV* 132–3). In such dialogues in the later family chronicles, Miss Yonge came to admit that young people's notions of heroism and social responsibility might take different directions from the ones she held dear, without necessarily being less worthy or sincere. There is a large-mindedness, with which she is not often credited, in what she wrote in *Womankind* when she was fifty-four.

> We enjoy progress as long as we go along with it, but . . . there often comes a time when the progress gets beyond this. And then! Are we to be drags, or stumbling-blocks, or to throw ourselves out of the course altogether? . . . Are these impertinent young things right or wrong? Or are they impertinent at all, and are we the ones in the wrong? . . . Each generation must think for itself . . . A welding together of the new and old is the thing needful, not that the old should

treat everything new as trumpery and mischievous, and the young everything old as worn out and ridiculous. It has been the strength and glory of England that she has built on her own foundations instead of sweeping them away; but when we pass the bound of our own youth, we have to bear in mind that it is narrow intolerance, on the part of the older generation, which provokes the younger into a general overthrow as soon as they have the power (WK 314–15, 319).

6

The Real Charlotte Yonge?

Miss Yonge's reputation and the circulation of her books remained high for most of her life. By 1868 *The Daisy Chain* was in its ninth edition, by 1876 *The Heir of Redclyffe* was in its twenty-second. A survey of schoolgirl readership in 1886 put Miss Yonge fourth on the list of favourite authors, after Dickens, Scott and Kingsley and just before Shakespeare.[1] As late as 1898 she was still high on the popularity poll of readers of the magazine *The Girls' Realm*.[2] Her works were widely read in other European countries; there were French, Spanish, Polish translations, and fan letters and signed photographs of royal readers reached her from Germany, Italy and Spain. One evidence of her European fame gave her real pleasure and amusement; an Italian newspaper announced – with a masterly confusion between the authoress, the title of her most famous book, and the name of Lord Stratford de Redcliffe, British Ambassador to Turkey –

> The celebrated English authoress, Era de Ratcliffe, has died. Her name was Jong, but in recognition of her talent, Queen Victoria made her a Viscountess.
> She married the British Ambassador to Constantinople, but she continued to write very beautiful novels till quite recently. (M and P 227)

Even in her own day, however, there were hostile critics. Dickens's magazine, *Household Words*, condemned her 'Pusey-stricken fancies' (KT 49–50). Mrs Austin mockingly declared herself unworthy of such 'superhuman flights of virtue in a novel', and young Hester Cholmondeley, of the very age and class most aimed at by

Miss Yonge, found all her stories 'too good, too dull and too High Church . . . I hate them'.[3] The Tractarian element in her novels became increasingly a bar between her and her readers, as she herself sadly acknowledged when at the very end of her life one of her children's stories failed to sell because, she surmised, it was 'too Churchy' (CC 346). By the early years of the twentieth century, writers of introductions to her books felt that they had to apologize for her old-fashioned values, or claim that one of her historical novels was 'refreshingly free from High Church proclivities' (this critic can hardly have read the book she was introducing, *The Dove in the Eagle's Nest*).[4] Other writers of children's books like E. Nesbit began to introduce mocking parodies of Miss Yonge's novels into their stories. An Oxford historian claimed that Miss Yonge's story-telling gift barely out-weighed her 'intolerable sententiousness and high-falutin' tone'.[5] The climax of hostile criticism of Miss Yonge, however, came from Cambridge, from Q. D. Leavis, in an astonishingly virulent review in *Scrutiny* of Georgina Battiscombe's biography of Miss Yonge. Outraged at the notion that 'the canon of English literature' might find itself burdened by a writer whom no critic could take seriously on literary grounds, she violently attacked Miss Yonge as 'living only in the ignorant idealization projected by an inhuman theory', her rigid interpretation of the Anglican faith. 'She has nothing to present but a moral ethos where everybody's first duty is to give up everything for everybody else and where no-one can enjoy anything without feeling guilty'. Mrs Leavis was using Charlotte Yonge partly as a stick with which to beat T. S. Eliot and C. S. Lewis, but her review, published in 1944, represents the nadir to which Miss Yonge's work fell in critical esteem.[6]

In fact it was at this point, during the War years of 1939–45 and the immediate post-war period, that interest in Miss Yonge's books began to take an upward turn. She had always continued to be cherished by a secret network of devoted readers, who responded with rapture to the discovery, from a series of events at this time, that they were not alone in their devotion. In 1939 the author E. M. Delafield wrote a letter to *The Times*, correcting a reference to Charlotte Yonge in a short article which *The Times* had previously published (BG 11). As a result E. M. Delafield received nearly 500 letters from habitual readers of Miss Yonge's books. In 1943 Georgina Battiscombe's *Charlotte Mary Yonge: The*

Story of an Uneventful Life – the first full biography since Christabel Coleridge's official *Life and Letters* in 1903 – was published, followed in 1947 by a second new biography, *Victorian Best-Seller: The World of Charlotte Yonge,* by Margaret Mare and Alicia Percival. In 1953 Professor Kathleen Tillotson gave a talk on the BBC Third Programme (later re-printed in her and her husband's *Mid-Victorian Studies*) to commemorate the centenary of the publication of *The Heir of Redclyffe.*

Miss Yonge had now emerged again from the hidden shrine where worshippers had guarded her for half a century. General literary historians began to ponder whether she had a real place in 'the canon of English literature', whether she pioneered any fictional techniques or influenced any successors. There was a changing attitude towards 'Victorian values', an emerging genera-tion no longer influenced by Lytton Strachey, and prepared to believe that writers whose opinions are no longer acceptable might nevertheless have held those opinions sincerely and without hypocrisy. The increasing number of historians of the Oxford Movement were interested in that aspect of Miss Yonge's work, which also began to impinge on the rising disciplines of female readership surveys and of the history of children's literature.

Above all, one critical section, the feminists – who already in the later years of the nineteenth century, especially in America, had aligned themselves against Miss Yonge – now began to take an increasingly direful interest in her novels. She was attacked as 'anti-feminist to the backbone' in 1966 by Patricia Thomson, who nevertheless suggested that it might soon be possible to judge novelists by other than feminist standards, but this prediction was prematurely hopeful. In 1977 Miss Yonge received a double blast, Anthea Zeiman inveighing against her for her defensive cult of filial obedience, while Elaine Showalter (whose knowledge of her subject's life can be gauged by her describing Miss Yonge's father as 'a rich clergyman') saw him as imposing disciplines and prohibitions on his daughter because he was afraid of her competing for dominance within the home, while she, aware of her father's jealous hostility to her work, developed a strategy of external submission which concealed a surreptitious pursuit of her own career and business interests. In 1981 J. S. Bratton found Miss Yonge's doctrine of female submission 'in the last degree un-reasonable, doctrinaire and repressive' and in 1987 Juliet

Dusinberre was still accusing Miss Yonge of hypocritically preaching what she did not practise.[7] A note of real hatred, of determination to find fault with every aspect of Miss Yonge's work, appears in some of these feminist criticisms, but some male critics throughout this century have also joined in the attack. Oliver Elton, for instance, considered that she treated female attempts to achieve independence with 'a really appalling harshness'.[8] Two characters in Miss Yonge's novels became feminist icons of martyrdom to male oppression: Ethel May in *The Daisy Chain*, a brilliantly clever girl morally blackmailed into giving up her beloved Greek studies to allow her more time for domestic and philanthropic duties, and Rachel Curtis in *The Clever Woman of the Family*, whose independent action to alleviate the lot of exploited child workers delivers her into the hands of a confidence trickster and ends in worsening the children's lot; she is contrasted with the submissive Ermine, who earns her own living by journalism, but secretly, not 'setting up for an authoress'. A few feminist critics like Catherine Sandbach-Dahlstrom have tried to elicit a more sympathetic 'muted' message of revolt against female submission, but in general Miss Yonge remains on the feminist blacklist.

It is undeniable that her ideas did not conform to many of those considered mandatory today. She was an élitist, taking class status and privileges for granted, convinced of the value of high birth and breeding – though not of wealth, she was not impressed by the nouveaux riches or even by inherited wealth and station in themselves; they could be justified only by the wise use made of them. She was a racist to the extent that she supported colonialism; she shows no signs of actual colour prejudice, and her *Book of Golden Deeds* celebrates Haitian and Sandwich Island heroes as well as European ones, but she probably never actually met a non-European other than the Queen of Honolulu, who once came to tea at Otterbourne. Elitism and racism were normal for people of her class and period, but her standpoint which will be thought most repugnant today, and which was in excess even of that of most of her contemporaries, was her male chauvinism, of which she was an uncompromising adherent. On the first page of her *Womankind*, a work anathema to any feminist critic, she said flatly 'I have no hesitation in declaring my full belief in the inferiority of woman, nor that she brought it upon herself . . . A woman of the highest faculties is of course superior to a man of the lowest; but she never attains to anything like the powers of a man of the highest ability' (*WK* 1–2). The consequence which she draws from this natural inequality is the still more unacceptable one that all women derive their thought and opinions from the man nearest to them. In *The Clever Woman of the Family*, the novel in which she exposes most completely her notion of woman's true role and place in society, she makes this doctrine explicit. 'A woman's tone of thought is commonly moulded by the masculine intellect which, under one form or another, becomes the master of her soul' (*CWF* 337). Her father and Keble had become the masters of *her* soul. The extent to which she accepted Keble's guidance about woman's role is ludicrously indicated by her anecdote about his corrections of her books; on one of them he commented 'It occurred to me whether, when the ladies quote Greek, they had not better say they have heard their fathers and brothers say things' (*MCY* pp. xxvi–xxvii).

It is not necessary to be an avowed feminist to be affronted by the degree of male chauvinism in Miss Yonge's novels. Even her most devoted admirers are shocked by the demands for womanly submission made throughout her works. Brothers as well as husbands and fathers are accorded the most despotic rights. They domineer over their sisters, exact their full-time attention, destroy their dolls, mock their feminine interests, and the sisters accept this with no sign of resentment, a serious flaw in her descriptions of sibling relationships, which in general are some of her most convincing successes. Husbands, even when they are portrayed as manifestly inferior in intellect to their wives, as with Mr and Mrs Edmondstone in *The Heir of Redclyffe*, or in moral stature as with the Ponsonbys in *Dynevor Terrace* or the Egremonts in *Nuttie's Father*, are deferred to with complete submission by their wives as well as their daughters. Above all, filial obedience is the strongest thread in the pattern of male dominance and female docility which is interwoven with all Miss Yonge's plots. Her novels portray all types of parents, from the noblest to the most fallible, from devouringly affectionate vampires to coldly unloving and aloof egoists, from austere scholars to dissolute men of the world, but filial submission to the worst as well as the best is regarded as an inescapable duty. Most critics have insisted that this exaggerated notion of parental authority and the duty of filial obedience was caused by the domination exercised on Miss Yonge herself by her father and Keble, which stunted her emotional growth, leaving her as a frustrated adolescent all her life.

Was she frustrated? It is a possibility that many critics have been eager to explore. Her first biographer, Christabel Coleridge (who committed the biographer's cardinal crime of destroying all her subject's letters and archives once she had used them herself) pronounced that 'No inconsistent nor disappointing record has, or ever can, leap to light where she was concerned' (CC p. v) – an almost irresistible challenge to later biographers to try to prove that Miss Yonge was sexually abused as a child by her father, hated her mother, had an illegitimate child by Keble, embezzled the funds of *The Monthly Packet* and plagiarized her plots from Eugène Sue. Some faint attempts have been made to debunk her character, to uncover an alternative 'real' Charlotte Yonge. It has been suggested on rather slight evidence that she was mean about money in small ways, though notoriously generous in large ones (BD 6–9, 21, 31–3). Her undoubted shyness and awkwardness, which sometimes repelled strangers, have been emphasized and traced to excessive parental discipline in youth. As a child she was allowed few indulgences, was scolded for the least inattention at her lessons, was laughed at for any trace of vanity or self-consequence, was forbidden to have any contact, other than school-teaching, with village neighbours. The strictness of her upbringing was thought excessive even by other contemporaries, but nearly all the evidence about it comes from her own auto-biographical recollections, and is related without a trace of resentment, indeed with gratitude. Neurosis-hunters could make a meal out of some of the anecdotes of her childhood, such as that she was naturally left-handed, but was disciplined into using her right hand instead, or that her favourite doll was confiscated and given away to a village child for fear its wooden head might damage her baby brother. What a repressed but seething brother-hatred could be deduced from that incident, except that Miss Yonge related it with amusement as part of an anecdote about the doll's subsequent part in cottage life. That, however, is not admitted as evidence of her sincerity and self-awareness by some of her critics, who explain it away as a front, a persona, a studied self-presentation to the outside world designed to protect the privacy of 'the real Charlotte Yonge' (BD 22). Subconsciously, it is suggested, she wanted to escape from her family into independence, but consciously she did not recognize her need for escape. When in her novels she reprobates women's claims to selfhood and independent status, she is unconsciously castigating tendencies within her own psyche.[9] The argument seems to be: she suffered severe discipline as a child; many girls would be made unhappy by such discipline, so she must have been unhappy; if she says that she was happy, she must therefore be concealing something. There are logical gaps in that sequence, but it is difficult for any post-Freudian critic to concede that training in self-control – regarded by Miss Yonge as one of the first of virtues – might be beneficial, not a synonym for repression. The main charge against her remains that of father-fixation, to Keble as well as to her real father, which stunted normal sexual development and thus produced unacknowledged but secretly working frustration, to be traced in coded messages throughout her novels.

Frustration is generally detectable in the lives of the frustrated by some signs of unhappiness or unbalance. It might be legitimate to surmise that Miss Yonge's life was maimed or ruined by parental domination if there were any signs that her life was maimed or ruined. In fact it was by all the evidence of herself and her contemporaries a happy and serene life. She was fully occupied by very successful work which she thoroughly enjoyed and believed to be a worthwhile moral mission. She was surrounded by the companionship of those whom she loved best. She had good health and no financial cares. She lived among the rural beauties which meant so much to her. Her only griefs were the natural losses of family and friends of an older generation, and the tragedy and trauma of such bereavement was mitigated by her firm belief in an after-life in which she would be re-united with loved ones. Her only tinge of bitterness and disappointment was a professional one when, late in her life, her books became less popular and she was deprived of the editorship of *The Monthly Packet* over which she had presided for so many years. There is no evidence at all, in her published works or her surviving letters, that she ever felt personal or sexual deprivation, except for one single remark. She told Elizabeth Wordsworth 'I have had a great deal of affection in my life, but not from the people I cared for most' (GB 103). There is no clue to the identity of the man or woman who failed to provide the love that she hoped for, but it cannot have been either her father or Keble, both of whom were devoted to her, and she probably was not referring to sexual love at all. Lewis Carroll, who met and photographed Miss Yonge in 1866, said 'I was very much pleased with her cheerful and easy manner', and thirty years later Mrs Sumner, founder of the Mothers' Union, who knew Miss Yonge in the last years of her life, said that she had 'no nervous excitability, no impatience or hurry in her work or manner . . . she had a quiet, cheerful, healthy, well-balanced mind' (CC 290). Those are not typical pictures of a frustrated woman. As one recent student of her works has pointed out, 'Again and again appreciative modern critics look in Miss Yonge's fiction for traces of suppressed hostilities and frustrated spinsterhood, but they never find anything at all convincing' (SD 106).

I suggest that Miss Yonge was a natural celibate – a phenomenon not as rare, even today, as is commonly believed – who was not much interested in sex. She observed its workings, as she observed everything, with a keen eye, and was quite able to convey a considerable erotic charge when describing the relationships of young married couples such as Arthur and Violet Martindale in *Heartsease* or Julius and Rosamond Charnock in *The Three Brides*. She observed sexual passion, as she observed other feelings in human beings which she herself did not share, or miss, or want – an ear for music, say, or a sea-going fancy, or a taste for fashionable clothes; feelings with which to equip her fictional characters, but neither good nor bad, desirable nor undesirable, in themselves, all that mattered to her was whether they were exercised or restrained under the rule of moral principle. She summarized her idea of the role of sexual passion in fiction in a letter to Mrs Humphry Ward, who had been ill-advised enough to submit a steamy story (about a hero who discovered his fiancée making love with a wicked baronet, and jumped off a cliff) to *The Monthly Packet*. Rejecting the story, Miss Yonge wrote 'I do not go on the principle of no love at all, and letting nobody marry, but I do not think it will do to have it the whole subject and interest of the story'.[10] There is no record of its emergence in her own real-life story; though she was pretty as a girl and handsome in middle age, brown-eyed, warm-complexioned and stately, though in conversation with friends she was cheerful and animated, there is no definite record that any man wanted to marry her. Perhaps she did have suitors whom she rejected. Perhaps she was too clever, too shy, too indifferent to her appearance, to have much sexual attraction for possible husbands of her own age. The only thing that seems clear is that sexual possibilities were far from being the most important thing in her life.

Some recent critics have conceded that, given Miss Yonge's special temperament, a non-sexual companionship with able and dominating elder men might be both intellectually and emotionally the most fulfilling destiny for her, and that she herself was quite aware of this. She certainly felt that her own shyness and awkwardness, which she admitted were due to the strict discipline of her childhood, were a small price to pay for the happy security of her family life. It was a conscious adult choice that the truthfulness and self-discipline imposed by her parents were of more value, a greater element of happiness, than the ease and self-assurance which a different upbringing might have conferred. Her critics tend to say that she never grew up, that emotionally she was a case of arrested development; but perhaps she did achieve adult fulfilment, only the filling was an unusual, but not therefore abnormal or immature, one. She opened her *Life of Bishop Patteson* with the statement that 'the happiest natures are generally those which have enjoyed the full benefit of parental training without dictation' (*LBP* vol 1, p. i); the happiest natures, not just the most virtuous, it should be noted – if she was at all a slave, she was a willing and enjoying slave. 'No-one ever had a happier or more joyous childhood than mine was' she claimed (CC 56–7). Her relationship to Keble was that of a disciple, a catechumen revering and loving a master priest, not that of a frustrated spinster with a father-fixation. She was quite aware of the danger of making idols, or 'Bilds' as she habitually called them, of anyone; her father was not her pope, she insisted.

The trouble was that she extrapolated from her own experience, peculiar to her special temperament, to thinking that such parental rule was mandatory for all women in all circumstances. It was sanctioned, in her view, by the Church, the ultimate authority which should govern all female endeavour. But her enthusiasm for male dominance remains an ugly inescapable blot on her picture of society, though she was not as consistently anti- feminist as has been suggested. She did not create, or admire, the really soft submissive helpless women, the Amelia Sedleys, preferred by the true male chauvinist. Even her most modest and shrinking heroines, like Violet Martindale in *Heartsease* or Christina in *The Dove in the Eagle's Nest*, have wills of iron when it comes to acting on their principles, even against masculine opposition.

Moreover her artistic integrity and fairness – sometimes at odds with her moral message – made her appreciate and portray the good qualities even of the over-independent self-sufficient feminists of whom she most disapproved. There is a fascinating portrait in *The Three Brides*, perhaps her most completely grown-up novel, of the American feminist Mrs Cleo W. Tallboys, who lectures on 'the claims of women, the inequality of social laws, the improvement of education, the comprehension of social science'. She is more used to holding forth than to rational argument ('I never was so interrupted' she complains, after a gripping diner-party conversation about woman's role), but she is beautifully dressed, can turn her hand to making delicious 'kickshaws' when her hostess's cook has let the side down, is polished and agreeable in ordinary conversation, and endures with good-humoured grace the mocking tactics of an anti-feminist family (*TB* 116, 137, 157–8, 162). Still more open-minded is Miss Yonge's admiring description of a young American girl in *The Trial*: 'A beautiful motherless girl, under seventeen – left, to all intents and purposes, alone in New York – attending a great educational establishment, far more independent and irresponsible than a young man at an English university, yet perfectly trustworthy . . . self-reliant, modest and graceful' (*TT* 280). She is not even as unfair to Rachel Curtis in *The Clever Woman of the Family* as has been maintained. Rachel is indeed represented as aggressively sure she is in the right, a poor judge of psychology, often absurd in her intellectual vanity, but also truthful, humble about her personal attractions, full of altruistic social concern, frankly and heartily ashamed when her mistakes lead to disaster. She is not the villainess of the story; that part is played by Bessie Keith, who charms everybody by her delightful gaiety and wit, but is a mischief-maker and a liar, who marries an elderly peer for his money and position but continues to flirt with a former lover. Rachel Curtis is favourably contrasted with Bessie, quite as much as she is unfavourably contrasted with the exemplary invalid authoress Ermine Williams.

Miss Yonge wanted women to be capable, even intellectual, so long as they did not assert their independence and self-sufficiency aggressively. If she did not think they should be encouraged to pursue Greek studies, like Ethel May, or authorship like Isabel Frost in *Dynevor Terrace*, at the expense of their domestic duties, she expected them to be a good deal more generally cultured and well-read than most of their counterparts are today. She approved of women like Ermine Williams, and Bessie Merrifield when she reappeared in the later family chronicles, who made a career by journalism or lecturing. She regarded efficient governesses like Mary Ogilvie in *Magnum Bonum* and Alison Williams in *The Clever Woman of the Family* as professionals, working women with a worthwhile job to do. Marilda Underwood in *The Pillars of the House* runs her father's City business after his death with sagacious confidence, and is approved for doing so. In later life Miss Yonge came to accept as inevitable the idea of secondary schools and public examinations and university education for women, even of women doctors. Her *Biographies of Good Women* included a surprising variety of teachers, actresses, poetesses, social workers, from Vittoria Colonna to Hannah More and from Dorothy Wordsworth to Mrs Siddons. She praised such a woman as the prison visitor and reformer Sarah Martin who, even before Elizabeth Fry, single-handedly created a new role for women. She could laugh approvingly when lauding the 'Golden Deed' of the housewives of Lowenberg who in 1611, by a sort of sit-in strike, cowed and defeated the male Town Council who were trying to force them to give up their Lutheran faith (*BGD* 253–60). 'It is the duty of a woman to make herself all that she can possibly be, and to work up her capabilities to the utmost that opportunity allows' she declared in a little-known novel of 1878, *The Disturbing Element*, but she added the proviso that it must be 'only for the sake of that love to God and her neighbours which finds its opportunities and channels in the charities of life'.

Some recent criticism has discerned that Miss Yonge was not rigidly opposed to any role for women as autonomous individuals, but was envisaging them as professionals in their own sphere, a sphere different from, but not inferior to, that of men.[11] Catherine Sandbach-Dahlstrom maintains that the women in Miss Yonge's novels who conform to the dominant ideology of female submission are in fact elevating woman's peculiar status. They stand for a value system, a 'self-worth', of their own. 'Her domestic angels are not primarily conjunct to men but occupy centres of interest in the novel and exert power and influence on all around them'. What is offered is a model of an ideal androgynous community in which the female virtues of compassion, sensitivity and self-sacrifice are adopted by men (SD 105, 107–8, 109, 129–37, 136, 163–8). A male critic, David Brownell, more moderately suggests that Ethel May, far from being exploited by a patriarchal society, has a fulfilled life as 'the most important person in the life of a superior man – her father' and in her responsibilities as head of the family and household.[12] Less preoccupation with the iniquities of the patriarchal society, more concentration on ways in which women establish their distinct worth and role, seem to be the directions of current feminist thinking by which Miss Yonge can now be judged.

Copies of Miss Yonge's books are now hard to come by. None are now in print, recent Virago reprints of *The Daisy Chain* and *The Clever Woman of the Family* having now been allowed to go out of print again. It is difficult to estimate how widespread her present readership is. While I was writing this study, and was often asked what I was currently working on, my mention of Charlotte Yonge often caused a glazed incomprehension to appear in the eyes of my questioners. On the other hand, when a well-known novelist claimed recently in a *Guardian* article to be the only person in England who read Miss Yonge's books, she aroused a chorus of amused protest; and when the *Observer* launched an appeal for the nomination of books that ought to be brought back into print, Miss Yonge's novels were among the suggestions received. There is one long-standing Charlotte Yonge Society, founded by a group of well-known authors and academics, and another is now being mooted.

It remains to be seen whether Miss Yonge's insistence on male and parental dominance will constitute an ever-rising barrier to present and future readership of her books, and whether an increasingly secularized public will be more and more alienated by religious elements which they find incomprehensible. She will continue to be read for pleasure, not now by the children and young girls for whom she mainly wrote, but by an adult readership of mainly middle-aged and elderly women, the real

'Codgerism'. Such a readership might suggest that her works should be relegated as the nineteenth-century equivalent of today's Aga-sagas; but that is as male-chauvinist a reaction as any of her own. Women readership is now a recognized topic for academic study, but Miss Yonge also qualifies in more general terms for the interest of students of the Victorian scene, which cannot be fully understood without some recognition of her influence on it. Mrs Leavis would have been horrified to hear that, fifty years after her diatribe, Miss Yonge has after all earned her place in 'the canon of English Literature'.

Notes

CHAPTER 1. STEERING THE READER: MISS YONGE'S LITERARY ART

1. *Uncollected Writings from 'Household Words', 1850–1859*, ed Harry Stone (Indiana University Press, 1968), vol 2, pp. 619–26.
2. Amy Cruse, *The Victorian and Their Books* (Allen & Unwin, 1935), 59.
3. *Alfred Lord Tennyson, a Memoir by His Son* (Macmillan, 1906), 456.
4. Oliver Elton, *A Survey of English Literature* (Edward Arnold, 1920), vol 2, pp. 304–6.
5. George Eliot, 'Silly Novels by Lady Novelists', *Westminster Review*, 66 (October 1856), 310–21.
6. Judith Rowbotham, *Good Girls Make Good Wives: Guidance for Girls in Victorian Fiction* (Blackwell, 1989), 151.
7. Juliet Dusinberre, *Alice to the Lighthouse: Children's Books and Radical Experiments in Art* (Macmillan, 1987), 132.
8. Anthea Zeman, *Presumptuous Girls: Women and Their World in the Serious Woman's Novel* (Weidenfeld & Nicolson, 1977), 18; Juliet Dusinberre, op cit, 66.

CHAPTER 2. FORMING THE READER: TRACTARIAN ROLE MODELS

1. Anne Dickenson, 'The Church in Miss Yonge's Novels', 10–14, in Charlotte M. Yonge Society Archives (see Select Bibliography).
2. Amy Cruse, op cit, 46, 425.
3. Mary Shakeshaft, 'Missions and Charities', 7-8, and Betty Askwith, 'Sisterhoods', 3–20, in Charlotte Mary Yonge Society Archives.
4. Mark Girouard, *The Return to Camelot: Chivalry and the English Gentleman* (York University Press, 1981), 172, 185, 250–1.
5. Alfred Tennyson, *In Memoriam*, st xxxiii.

CHAPTER 3. ICONS AND STEREOTYPES

1. Anna Jameson, 'On the Relative Social Position of Mothers and Governesses, in *Memoirs and Essays* (Richard Boutley, 1846).

CHAPTER 4. HISTORICAL IMAGINATION

1. C. A. E. Moberly, *Dulce Domum: George Moberly, His Family and Friends* (John Murray, 1911), 60.
2. Juliet Dusinberre, op cit, 66.
3. E. C. Withycombe, *Oxford Dictionary of English Christian Names*, (Clarendon Press, 1945), p. iii.

CHAPTER 5. SOCIAL CHANGE: NOSTALGIA AND ACCEPTANCE

1. Georgina Battiscombe, *John Keble: A Study in Limitatons* (Constable, 1963), 274.

CHAPTER 6. THE REAL CHARLOTTE YONGE?

1. Edward G. Salmon, 'What Girls Read', *Nineteenth Century*, 20 (October 1886), 519–29.
2. Mary Cadogan and Patricia Craig, *You're a Brick, Angela: A New Look at Girls' Fiction from 1839 to 1975* (Gollancz, 1976), 55.
3. Amy Cruse, op cit, 55, 59.
4. Alice Meynell, Introduction, *The Heir of Redclyffe* (Everyman, 1909); E. Hull, Introduction, *The Dove in the Eagle's Nest* (Everyman, 1908).
5. E. M. Jamieson in Georgina Battiscombe, *Reluctant Pioneer* (Constable, 1978, 261.
6. Q. D. Leavis, 'Charlotte Yonge and Christian Discrimination', *Scrutiny*, 12 (1944), 153–9.
7. Patricia Thomson, *The Victorian Heroine: A Changing Ideal, 1837–1873* (Oxford University Press, 1956), 61–3, 166; Anthea Zeman, op cit, 18; Elaine Showalter, *A Literature of Their Own: British Women Novelists from Brontë to Lessing* (Princeton University Press, 1977), 56–7; J. S. Bratton, *The Impact of Victorian Children's Fiction* (Croom Helm, 1981), 182; Juliet Dusinberre, op cit, 66.
8. Oliver Elton, op cit, vol 2, pp. 304–6.
9. David Brownell, 'The Two Worlds of Charlotte Yonge', *The Worlds of Victorian Fiction*, ed J. H. Buckley, *Harvard English Studies*, 6,

(Harvard University Press, 1975), 166–78; Juliet Dusinberre, op cit, 84; J. S. Bratton, op cit, 188–9.

10. John Sutherland, *Mrs Humphry Ward* (Clarendon Press, 1990), 38–9.
11. Judith Rowbotham, op cit, 266; Gillian Avery, *Childhood's Pattern: A Study of the Heroes and Heroines of Children's Fiction, 1770–1950* (Hodder & Stoughton, 1975), 200.
12. David Brownell, op cit, 166–78.

Select Bibliography

BIBLIOGRAPHIES AND REFERENCE WORKS

No complete bibliography of all Miss Yonge's novels, short stories, articles, book reviews, translations, introductions, and contributions to symposia has yet been published. Titles of her book-length publications have been variously estimated at 120, 160, 184, or 250, and many of these have been constantly re- issued, in at least 1,000 editions. In all, she is estimated to have published fifteen million words.

Drazin, P. G., *Bibliography of Works and Translations by Charlotte Yonge and of Critical Studies of Her Work.* (Unpublished. Applications for access to this, the most complete bibliography of Charlotte Yonge, should be made to Professor P. G. Drazin, School of Mathematics, University of Bristol, University Walk, Bristol BS8 1TW.)

Dunlap, Barbara, 'Selected Books by Charlotte Mary Yonge', in *Dictionary of Literary Biography: Victorian Novelists after 1885*, ed Ira B. Nadel and William E. Fredman (Gale Research Company, 1983), 308–11.

Laski, Marghanita, and Kathleen Tillotson, Bibliography in *A Chaplet for Charlotte Yonge* (Cresset Press, 1965), 204–16.

SELECTED WORKS BY CHARLOTTE YONGE

(all published in London unless otherwise stated)

Abbeychurch, or Self-Control and Self-Conceit (Burns, 1844).

Armourer's Apprentice, The (Macmillan, 1884).

'Authorship', in *Ladies at Work: Papers on Paid Employment for Ladies* (Innes, 1893) and *A Chaplet for Charlotte Yonge*, 185–92

Beechcroft at Rockstone (Macmillan, 1888).

Book of Golden Deeds of All Times and All Lands, A (Macmillan, 1864).

Book of Worthies, Gathered from the Old Histories and Now Written Anew (Macmillan, 1869).

Bye-Words: A Collection of Tales New and Old (Macmillan, 1880).

Caged Lion, The (Macmillan, 1870).

Cameos from English History, 9 vols (Macmillan, 1868–99).

Carbonels, The (National Society's Depository, 1896).

Castle Builders, The, or The Deferred Confirmation (Mozley, 1854).

Chantry House (Macmillan, 1886).

Chaplet of Pearls, The, or The White and the Black Ribaumont (Macmillan, 1868).

Château de Melville, Le (Winchester: Jacob & Johnson, 1839).

'Children's Literature of the Last Century', in *Macmillan's Magazine*, 20 (July to October 1869), 229–37, 302–10, 448–56.

Clever Woman of the Family, The (Macmillan, 1865).

'Come to Her Kingdom', *More Bywords* (Macmillan, 1890) and *A Chaplet for Charlotte Yonge*, 152–80.

Conversations on the Catechism, 3 vols (Mozley, 1859–63).

Countess Kate (Mozley, 1882).

Daisy Chain, The or Aspirations: A Family Chronicle (Parker, 1856).

Danvers Papers, The: an Invention (Macmillan, 1867).

Disturbing Element, The, or Chronicles of the Bluebell Society (Ward, 1878).

Dove in the Eagle's Nest, The (Macmillan, 1866).

Dynevor Terrace, or The Clue of Life (Parker, 1857).

Founded on Paper, or Uphill and Downhill Between the Two Jubilees (National Society's Depository, 1898).

Grisly Grisell, or the Laidly Lady of Whitburn: A Tale of the Wars of the Roses (Macmillan, 1893).

Heartsease, or The Brother's Wife (Parker, 1854).

Heir of Redclyffe, The (Parker, 1853).

Henrietta's Wish, or Domineering (Macmillan, 1850).

History of Christian Names, A 2 vols (Parker, 1863; revised edition, Macmillan, 1884).

Hopes and Fears, or Scenes from the Life of a Spinster (Parker, 1860).

Kenneth, or the Rear Guard of the Grand Army (Parker, 1850).

Lady Hester, or Ursula's Narrative (Macmillan, 1874).

Lances of Lynwood, The (Parker, 1855).

'Last Heartsease Leaves', in *Events of the Month*, January 1865, and *A Chaplet for Charlotte Yonge*, 129–138.

Life of John Coleridge Patteson, Missionary Bishop of the Melanesian Islands, 2 vols (Macmillan, 1874).

'Link between *The Castle Builders* and *The Pillars of the House*, A', in *The Monthly Packet*, December 1871, and *A Chaplet for Charlotte Yonge*, 139–51.

Little Duke, The, or Richard the Fearless (Parker, 1854).

Long Vacation, The (Macmillan, 1895).

Love and Life: An Old Story in Eighteenth Century Costume (Macmillan, 1880).

Magnum Bonum, or Mother Carey's Brood (Macmillan, 1879).

Modern Broods, or Developments Unlooked For (Macmillan, 1900).

Modern Telemachus, A (Macmillan, 1886).

More Bywords (Macmillan, 1890).

Musings Over 'The Christian Year' and 'Lyra Innocentium', Together with a few Gleanings of Recollections of the Rev John Keble, Gathered by Several Friends (Parker, 1874).

My Young Alcides: A Faded Photograph (Macmillan, 1875).

New Ground: Kaffirland (Morley, 1868).

Nuttie's Father (Macmillan, 1885).

Old Woman's Outlook in a Hampshire Village, An (Macmillan, 1892).

P's and Q's, or The Question of Putting Upon (Macmillan, 1872).

Pigeon Pie, The (Mozley, 1860).

Pilgrimage of Ben Beriah (Macmillan, 1897).

Pillars of the House, The, or Under Wode, Under Rode, 2 vols (Macmillan, 1873).

Prince and the Page, The: A Story of the Last Crusade (Macmillan, 1866).

Reasons Why I Am A Catholic and Not A Roman Catholic (Wells Gardner, 1901).

Release, The, or Caroline's French Kindred (Macmillan, 1896).

Reputed Changeling, A, or Three Seventh Years Two Centuries Ago (Macmillan, 1889).

Scenes and Characters, or Eighteen Months at Beechcroft (Mozley, 1847).

Stokesley Secret, The (Mozley, 1861).

Stray Pearls: Memoirs of Margaret de Ribaumont, Viscountess of Bellaise (Macmillan, 1883).

Strolling Players: A Harmony of Contrasts (with Christabel Coleridge) (Macmillan, 1893).

That Stick, 2 vols (Macmillan, 1892).

Three Brides, The (Macmillan, 1876).

Treasures in the Marshes, The (National Society's Depository, 1893).

Trial, The: More Links of The Daisy Chain (Macmillan, 1864).

Two Guardians, The, or Home in This World (Macmillan, 1852).

Two Penniless Princesses (Macmillan, 1891).

Two Sides of the Shield, The (Macmillan, 1885).

Unknown to History: A Story of the Captivity of Mary of Scotland (Macmillan, 1882).

Village Children, ed Gillian Avery (Gollancz, 1967).

What Books to Lend and What to Give (National Society's Depository, 1887).

Womankind (Walter Smith, 1877).
Young Stepmother, The, or A Chronicle of Mistakes (Longman, 1861).

CRITICAL AND BIOGRAPHICAL STUDIES

Note: CMYS Archives = Unpublished papers read to the Charlotte M. Yonge Society, 1965–95. Photocopies of this copyright material cannot be supplied, but written applications for access to them by qualified researchers may be made to The Hon Secretary, Charlotte M. Yonge Society, Flat 3, 18 Belsize Grove, London NW3 4UN.

Askwith, Betty, 'Sisterhoods and Charlotte M. Yonge', CMYS Archives.
Battiscombe, Georgina, *Charlotte Mary Yonge: the Story of an Uneventful Life* (Constable, 1943). The standard modern biography, which did much to revive interest in Miss Yonge and her work.
—ed (with Marghanita Laski), *A Chaplet for Charlotte Yonge* (Cresset Press, 1965). Contains papers read to the Charlotte M. Yonge Society 1961–5 by Elizabeth Jenkins, Lettice Cooper, Margaret Kennedy and others, reprints of short pieces by Miss Yonge linking her family chronicles, genealogical trees of her fictional families, and a bibliography of her works.
Briggs, Katharine M., *Folklore in the Works of Charlotte Yonge*, ed Kathleen Tillotson (Occasional Papers of the K. B. Club, 1990).
Brownell, David, 'The Two Worlds of Charlotte Yonge', in *The Worlds of Victorian Fiction*, ed J. H. Buckley, Harvard English Studies, 6, (Harvard: Harvard University Press, 1975), 166–78.
Coleridge, Christabel, *Charlotte Mary Yonge. Her Life and Letters* (Macmillan, 1903). The first, official, biography. Uncritical, but full of valuable details.
Dennis, Barbara, *Charlotte Yonge (1823–1901), Novelist of the Oxford Movement: a Literature of Victorian Customs and Society* (Lampeter: Edwin Mellen Press, 1992). The fullest survey of Miss Yonge in the Tractarian context.
Dickenson, Anne, 'The Church in Charlotte Yonge's Novels', CMYS Archives.
Dunlap, Barbara J., 'Charlotte Mary Yonge', in *Victorian Novelists after 1855*, ed Ira Nadel and W. E. Fredman, *Dictionary of Literary Biography*, 18 (Detroit: Gale Research Company, 1983), 308–25.
—'How the Victorians Viewed Miss Yonge; Some Contemporary Reviews of Her Domestic Novels', CMYS Archives.
Fischel, Katie, 'History: Its Scope, Purpose and Strength in the Novels of Charlotte Yonge', CMYS Archives.

Haldane, Charlotte, Preface to *The Heir of Redclyffe* (Duckworth, 1964).

Hayter, Alethea, 'The Sanitary Idea and a Victorian Novelist', in *History Today*, 19: 12 (December 1969), 840–7.

—'Authors and Authorship in Miss Yonge's Novels', CMYS Archives.

—'Mourning and Funeral Customs in Charlotte Yonge's Novels', CMYS Archives.

Hutton, R. H., 'Ethical and Dogmatic Fiction: Miss Yonge', in *National Review*, 12 (1861), 211–30.

Leavis, Q. D., 'Charlotte Yonge and Christian Discrimination', in *Scrutiny*, 12: 2 (Spring 1944), 152–80.

Mare, Margaret, and Alicia C. Percival, *Victorian Best-Seller: The World of Charlotte M. Yonge* (Harrap, 1947). Contains much useful background material on nineteenth-century customs and values.

Meynell, Alice, Introduction to *The Heir of Redclyffe* (Everyman, 1909).

Romanes, Ethel, *Charlotte M. Yonge: an Appreciation* (Mowbray, 1908). The first literary criticism of Miss Yonge's work.

Sandbach-Dahlstrom, Catherine, *Be Good Sweet Maid: Charlotte Yonge's Domestic Fiction: A Study in Dogmatic Purpose and Fictional Form* (Stockholm: Almqvist & Wiskell, 1984). A detailed deconstruction of Miss Yonge's literary art and themes.

Shakeshaft, Mary, 'Missions and Charities in the Novels of Charlotte Mary Yonge', CMYS Archives.

BACKGROUND READING

Avery, Gillian, *Childhood's Pattern: A Study of the Heroes and Heroines of Children's Fiction, 1770–1950* (Hodder & Stoughton, 1975).

Battiscombe, Georgina, *John Keble. A Study in Limitations* (Constable, 1963).

—*Reluctant Pioneer: A Life of Elizabeth Wordsworth* (Constable, 1978).

Bratton, J. S., *The Impact of Victorian Children's Fiction* (Croom Helm, 1981).

Cadogan, Mary, and Patricia Craig, *You're A Brick, Angela; A New Look at Girls' Fiction from 1839 to 1975* (Gollancz, 1976).

Chapman, Raymond, *Faith and Revolt: Studies in the Literary Influence of the Oxford Movement* (Weidenfeld and Nicolson, 1970).

Cruse, Amy, *The Victorians and Their Books* (Allen & Unwin, 1935).

Darton, F. J. Harvey, *Children's Books in England; Five Centuries of Social Life* (Cambridge University Press, 1982).

Dusinberre, Juliet, *Alice to the Lighthouse: Children's Books and Radical Experiment in Art* (Macmillan, 1987).

Elton, Oliver, *A Survey of English Literature*, 2 vols (Edward Arnold, 1920).

Flint, Kate, *The Woman Reader, 1817–1914* (Clarendon Press, 1993).

Moberly, C. A. E., *Dulce Domum: George Moberly, His Family and Friends* (John Murray, 1911).

Rowbotham, Judith, *Good Girls Make Good Wives: Guidance for Girls in Victorian Fiction* (Blackwell, Oxford, 1989).

Salmon, Edward G., 'What Girls Read', in *Nineteenth Century*, 20 (October 1886), 515–29.

Showalter, Elaine, *A Literature of Their Own: British Women Novelists from Brontë to Lessing* (Princeton: Princeton University Press, 1977).

Thomson, Patricia, *The Victorian Heroine. A Changing Ideal, 1837–1873* (Oxford University Press, 1956).

Thwaite, M. F., *From Primer to Pleasure: an Introduction to the History of Children's Books in England* (Library Association, 1963).

Tillotson, Kathleen, *Mid-Victorian Studies* (Athlone Press 1965).

Zeman, Anthea, *Presumptuous Girls: Women and Their World in the Serious Woman's Novel* (Weidenfeld and Nicolson, 1977).

Index

Alcott, Louisa, 2
Arnold, Matthew, 39
Austen, Jane, 2, 3, 4, 7, 8, 10, 38
  Sense and Sensibility, 5
Austin, Sarah, 54
Avery, Gillian, 48

Balzac, Honoré de, 2
Barter, Warden, 19
Battiscombe, Georgina, 55–6, 73
Beach, Mrs Hicks, *Amabel and
  Mary Verena*, 4
Bratton, J. S., 56
Briggs, Katharine M., 4, 46, 73
Brontë, Anne, 35
Brontë, Charlotte, 23, 39
  Jane Eyre, 23, 30–1, 34
  Shirley, 49
  Villette, 1
Broughton, Rhoda, 2
Brownell, David, 65
Browning, Elizabeth Barrett, 6
Bulwer Lytton, Edward, 47
Bunyan, John, 39
Burne-Jones, Edward, 2, 7, 23
Butterfield, William, 3, 22
Byron, George Gordon Lord, 39

Carlyle, Jane Welsh, 6
Carlyle, Thomas, 20, 26, 39
Carroll, Lewis, 1, 39, 61
Cattermole, George, 30

Chapman, Raymond, 7, 8
Charlotte M. Yonge Society, 65,
  73
Cholmondeley, Hester, 54–5
Coleridge, Christabel, 56, 59, 73
Coleridge, Judge, 1
Collier, John, 29, 36
Collins, Wilkie, 2
Collinson, James, 29
Colonna, Vittoria, 64
Cooper, Lettice, 6, 73

Dante Alighieri, 38
Darwin, Charles, 26
Delafield, E. M., 55
Dennis, Barbara, 16, 23, 73
Dickens, Charles, 6, 39, 54
  Bleak House, 1, 23
  David Copperfield, 15, 29, 37
  Dombey and Son, 32
  Martin Chuzzlewit, 34
  Old Curiosity Shop, The, 30, 32
  Our Mutual Friend, 39
Dumas, Alexandre, 39
Dusinberre, Juliet, 57
Dyson, Marianne, 17, 18

Egg, Augustus, 29
Eliot, George, 1, 10–11, 13, 19, 39
  Adam Bede, 2
  Daniel Deronda, 19
  Middlemarch, 37, 49

Mill on the Floss, The, 35
  Silas Marner, 25
Eliot, T. S., 55
Elton, Oliver, 8, 57
Ewing, Juliana Horatia, 32

Feminist Criticism, 13–4, 56–65
Fitzgerald, Edward, 2
Flaubert, Gustave, 2
Freeman, E. A., 40
Froude, Hurrell, 5
Froude, James Anthony, 26
Fry, Elizabeth, 64

Gaskell, Elizabeth, 8, 32, 39
  North and South, 1
  Ruth, 35
Gladstone, William Ewart, 1
Girouard, Mark, 23
Green, J. R., 40
Greenaway, Kate, 29
Guizot, Francois, 1

Haggard, H. Rider, 39
Heathcote, Sir William, 17
Hughes, Arthur, 29
Hunt, Holman, 29

Ingelow, Jean, 34

James, Henry, 18, 43
Jameson, Anna, 36
Johnson, Samuel, 39

Keble, Rev. John, 1, 3, 9, 16–17,
    18, 19, 38, 44, 45, 49, 58, 60,
    61, 62
  Christian Year, The, 17, 39
Kingsley, Charles, 1, 39, 54

Lawrence, George, 2
Leavis, Q. D., 55, 66
Lewes, G. H., 1

Lewis, C. S., 41, 55
Lyttelton, Lucy, 20

Macaulay, Thomas Babington, 44
Malory, Sir Thomas, 5
Manzoni, Alessandro, 38
Mare, Margaret, 56, 74
Martin, Sarah, 64
Martineau, Harriet, 12, 34
Martineau, R. B., 29, 30
Millais, John Everett, 29, 32
Missions and Missionaries, 21–5,
    27, 47
Moberly, Anne, 52
Moberly, Bishop George, 3, 5,
    17
Monthly Packet, The, 21, 24, 26,
    39, 43, 51, 60, 61
More, Hannah, 64
Morris, William, 2, 7

Nesbit, E., 55

Oliphant, Margaret, 2, 25
Otterbourne, 16, 22, 48, 51, 57
Oxford Movement, see under
    Tractarianism

Palgrave, Francis, 3
Patteson, Bishop John Coleridge,
    1, 9, 24
Percival, Alicia, 56, 74
Plutarch, 43
Pre-Raphaelite Brotherhood, 2, 7
Puseyism, see under
    Tractarianism

Raglan, Lord, 1
Raverat, Gwen, 14
Redgrave, Richard, 34, 35
Richardson, Samuel, 19
Romanes, Ethel, 3, 20, 28, 51, 74
Rossetti, Christina, 1

Rossetti, Dante Gabriel, 7
Ruskin, John, 23

Saintsbury, George, 2
Sandbach-Dahlstrom, Catherine, 13, 57, 64–5, 74
Sant, James, 30, 32
Scott, Sir Walter, 38, 41, 43, 54
Seaton, Lord, 19
Shakespeare, William, 38, 54
Shelley, Percy Bysshe, 39
Sherwood, Mary, 10, 27, 32
Showalter, Elaine, 56
Siddons, Sarah, 64
Sidgwick, Henry, 2
Sisterhoods, 22–3, 25
Slessor, Rev. John Henry, 22
Southey, Robert, 13
Spenser, Edmund, 38
Stephen, Fitzjames, 2
Stevenson, Robert Louis, 39
Strachey, Lytton, 56
Stratford de Redcliffe, Lord, 54
Street, G. E., 22
Sumner, Mrs, 61
Surtees, R. S., 1

Tait, Archbishop, 6
Thackeray, William Makepeace, 34, 39
  Newcomes, The, 1
  Pendennis, 15, 37
  Vanity Fair, 34, 49, 63

Thomson, Patricia, 56
Tillotson, Kathleen, 19, 39, 56
Tractarianism, 2, 7, 16–28, 49, 54, 55, 56
Trollope, Anthony, 1, 2, 4, 39
  Barchester Towers, 26
  Warden, The, 1

Ward, Mrs Humphry, 26, 61

White, Gilbert, 46
Wood, Mrs Henry, 2, 35
Wordsworth, Dorothy, 64
Wordsworth, Elizabeth, 5, 52, 60
Wordsworth, William, 38

Yonge, Charlotte: Anti-feminism, and depreciation by feminist critics, 13, 14, 56–65; criticism of other writers, 7, 8, 10–11, 12, 39–40; family chronicle formula, 4–6, 42, 58; historical and biographical approach, 9, 20, 40–45; influence, creation of role models, 2, 19–21, 23–5, 27–8, 37, 39, 40, 42, 43–4; literary standing and readership, in her own day, 1, 2–3, 4, 12, 20–1, 39, 42–3; 48; after her death, 4, 54–7, 65–6; literary techniques, 4–15, 19, 31, 33, 40, 41–2, 45; observation of social change, 17–18, 48–53; personality, 59–65; relationship with her father, 16, 38, 49, 56, 58, 59, 60, 61, 62; religious beliefs and aims, 13, 14, 16–28, 49, 51, 55, 65
Works: *Abbeychurch*, 18; *Aunt Charlotte's Stories of American etc History*, 43; *Beechcroft at Rockstone*, 4, 51; *Biographies of Good Women*, 20, 40, 43, 64; *Book of Golden Deeds, A*, 1, 20, 23, 44, 57, 64; *Book of Worthies, A*, 20; *Cameos from History*, 43; *Carbonels, The*, 49–50; *Castle Builders, The*, 3, 18; *Chaplet of Pearls, The*, 1, 7, 42; *Clever Woman of the Family, The*, 58, 65, Curtis,

Rachel, 10, 26, 57, 63, Keith,
Bessie, 63, Temple Fanny,
10, Williams, Ermine, 57, 63,
64, Williams, Alison, 64;
Come to her Kingdom, 4;
*Conversations on the
Catechism*, 21, 40; *Countess
Kate*, 3, 5, 11; *Daisy Chain,
The*, 1, 2, 3, 6, 7, 19. 21–2,
24, 36, 51, 54, May, Ethel, 3,
5, 19, 20, 36, 57, 64, 65, May,
Flora, 19, May, Norman, 24,
27, May, Dr Richard, 3, 11,
36, 65; *Disturbing Element,
The*, 64; *Dove in the Eagle's
Nest, The*, 7, 42, 55,
Christina, 63; *Dynevor
Terrace*, 58, 64; *Founded on
Paper*, 44, 50; *Heartsease*, 1, 3,
7, 10, 20, 22, 32, Martindale,
Arthur, 37, 61, Martindale,
John, 7, Martindale, Johnny,
32, Martindale, Violet, 7, 37,
61, 63; *Heir of Redclyffe, The*,
1, 3, 7, 14, 18–19, 20, 32, 43,
46, 54, 56, 58, Edmondstone,
Amy, 7, 29, 32, Morville,
Guy, 2, 3, 5, 7, 19, 27, 29, 32,
Morville, Philip, 7, 18, 46;
Henrietta's Wish, 18; *History
of Christian Names*, 45–6;
Hopes and Fears, 7, 20, 21, 24,
31–7, Charlecote, Honora 5,
31–3, 52, Fennimore, Miss,
34, 35–6, Fulmort, Bertha,
26, Fulmort, Maria, 35–6,
Fulmort, Mervyn, 37,
Fulmort, Phoebe, 33, 35,
Fulmort, Robert, 21, 33,
Raymond, Cecily, 37,
Sandbrook, Owen, 31–3;
Landmarks of History, 43,
Langley School, 48; *Last

Heartsease Leaves, 3; *Life of
Bishop Patteson*, 14, 44–5, 62;
*Link between the Castle
Builders and The Pillars of the
House, A*, 3; *Little Duke, The*,
19, 42; *Long Vacation, The*, 4,
24, 25, 51; Merrifield, Lilias,
52; *Love and Life*, 41, 46;
Magnum Bonum, 7, 38,
Brownlow, Barbara, 26,
Brownlow Bobus, 27,
Ogilvie, Mary, 64; *Making of
a Missionary, The*, 24; *Modern
Broods*, 4, 22, 51, 52; *Modern
Telemachus, A*, 46; *Musings
on 'The Christian Year'*, 9, 17,
40; *My Young Alcides*, 46;
New Ground, 19, 24, 47;
Nuttie's Father, 58; *Old
Woman's Outlook on a
Hampshire Village, An*, 46–7;
*Pilgrimage of the Ben Beriah,
The*, 41; *Pillars of the House,
The*, 3, 7, 9, 21, 22, 23, 32,
38, Underwood, Angela,
25–6, Underwood, Edgar, 9,
27, Underwood, Edward, 17,
Underwood, Felix, 9, 14, 19,
27, 52, Underwood, Gerald,
24, Underwood, Geraldine,
7, 11, Underwood, Marilda,
64, Underwood, Theodore,
32; *Reputed Changeling, A*,
46; *Scenes and Characters*, 3,
5, 18; *Stokesley Secret, The*, 3;
Strolling Players, 4; *Three
Brides, The*, 18, 19, 23, 51,
Charnock, Rosamond and
Julius, 61, Tallboys, Mrs
Cleo, 63; *Treasures in the
Marshes, The*, 49; *Trial, The*,
2, 3, 21, 23, 38, 40–1, 51, 63;
Two Sides of the Shield, The,

4, 30, Merrifield, Bessie, 5,
10, 64; *Unknown to History*,
11, 40; *What Books to Lend,
and What to Give*, 39; *Why I
Am a Catholic and Not a
Roman Catholic*, 18;
Womankind, 12, 34, 52–3,
57–8; *Young Stepmother, The*,
3, 7, 51

Yonge, Fanny, 3, 16
Yonge, Dr James, 36
Yonge, Julian, 59
Yonge, William, 16, 17, 22, 38,
56, 58, 59, 60, 61, 62

Zeiman, Anthea, 56
Zola, Emile, 2

*Recent and
Forthcoming Titles
in the
New Series of*

WRITERS AND
THEIR WORK

---

*"...this series promises to outshine its own
previously high reputation."*
Times Higher Education Supplement

*"...will build into a fine multi-volume critical
encyclopaedia of English literature."*
Library Review & Reference Review

"...Excellent, informative, readable, and recommended."
NATE News

"...promises to be a rare series of creative scholarship."
Times Educational Supplement

RECENT & FORTHCOMING TITLES

Title	Author
W.H. Auden	*Stan Smith*
Aphra Behn	*Sue Wiseman*
Lord Byron	*J. Drummond Bone*
Angela Carter	*Lorna Sage*
Geoffrey Chaucer	*Steve Ellis*
Children's Literature	*Kimberley Reynolds*
John Clare	*John Lucas*
Joseph Conrad	*Cedric Watts*
John Donne	*Stevie Davies*
Henry Fielding	*Jenny Uglow*
Elizabeth Gaskell	*Kate Flint*
William Golding	*Kevin McCarron*
Graham Greene	*Peter Mudford*
Hamlet	*Ann Thompson & Neil Taylor*
Thomas Hardy	*Peter Widdowson*
David Hare	*Jeremy Ridgman*
Tony Harrison	*Joe Kelleher*
William Hazlitt	*J.B. Priestley; R.L. Brett (introduction by Michael Foot)*
Seamus Heaney	*Andrew Murphy*
George Herbert	*T.S. Eliot (introduction by Peter Porter)*
Henry James - The Later Writing	*Barbara Hardy*
James Joyce	*Steven Connor*
King Lear	*Terence Hawkes*
Doris Lessing	*Elizabeth Maslen*
David Lodge	*Bernard Bergonzi*
Christopher Marlowe	*Thomas Healy*
Andrew Marvell	*Annabel Patterson*
Ian McEwan	*Kiernan Ryan*
A Midsummer Night's Dream	*Helen Hackett*
Walter Pater	*Laurel Brake*
Jean Rhys	*Helen Carr*
Dorothy Richardson	*Carol Watts*
The Sensation Novel	*Lyn Pykett*
Edmund Spenser	*Colin Burrow*
J.R.R. Tolkien	*Charles Moseley*
Leo Tolstoy	*John Bayley*
Virginia Woolf	*Laura Marcus*
Charlotte Yonge	*Alethea Hayter*

TITLES IN PREPARATION

Title	Author
Peter Ackroyd	*Susana Onega*
Antony and Cleopatra	*Ken Parker*
Jane Austen	*Robert Clark*
Samuel Beckett	*Keir Elam*
William Blake	*John Beer*
Elizabeth Bowen	*Maud Ellmann*
Emily Brontë	*Stevie Davies*
A.S. Byatt	*Richard Todd*
Caryl Churchill	*Elaine Aston*
S.T. Coleridge	*Stephen Bygrave*
Crime Fiction	*Martin Priestman*
Charles Dickens	*Rod Mengham*
Carol Ann Duffy	*Deryn Rees Jones*
Daniel Defoe	*Jim Rigney*
George Eliot	*Josephine McDonagh*
E.M. Forster	*Nicholas Royle*
Brian Friel	*Geraldine Higgins*
Henry IV	*Peter Bogdanov*
Henrik Ibsen	*Sally Ledger*
Rudyard Kipling	*Jan Montefiore*
Franz Kafka	*Michael Wood*
John Keats	*Kelvin Everest*
Philip Larkin	*Laurence Lerner*
D.H. Lawrence	*Linda Ruth Williams*
Measure for Measure	*Kate Chedgzoy*
William Morris	*Anne Janowitz*
Brian Patten	*Linda Cookson*
Alexander Pope	*Pat Rogers*
Sylvia Plath	*Elizabeth Bronfen*
Richard II	*Margaret Healy*
Lord Rochester	*Peter Porter*
Romeo and Juliet	*Sasha Roberts*
Christina Rossetti	*Kathryn Burlinson*
Salman Rushdie	*Damian Grant*
Sir Walter Scott	*John Sutherland*
Stevie Smith	*Alison Light*
Wole Soyinka	*Mpalive Msiska*
Laurence Sterne	*Manfred Pfister*
Jonathan Swift	*Claude Rawson*
The Tempest	*Gordon McMullan*
Mary Wollstonecraft	*Jane Moore*
Evelyn Waugh	*Malcolm Bradbury*
John Webster	*Thomas Sorge*
Angus Wilson	*Peter Conradi*
William Wordsworth	*Nicholas Roe*
Working Class Fiction	*Ian Haywood*
W.B. Yeats	*Ed Larrissy*